1950s Rock

52 TOP GUITAR HITS OF THE DECADE

ISBN 978-1-4234-8937-5

Visit Hal Leonard Online at
www.halleonard.com

Contact Us:
Hal Leonard
7777 West Bluemound Road
Milwaukee, WI 53213
Email: info@halleonard.com

In Europe contact:
Hal Leonard Europe Limited
Distribution Centre, Newmarket Road
Bury St Edmunds, Suffolk, IP33 3YB
Email: info@halleonardeurope.com

In Australia contact:
Hal Leonard Australia Pty. Ltd.
4 Lentara Court
Cheltenham, Victoria, 3192 Australia
Email: info@halleonard.com.au

STRUM AND PICK PATTERNS

This chart contains the suggested strum and pick patterns that are referred to by number at the beginning of each song in this book. The symbols ⊓ and ∨ in the strum patterns refer to down and up strokes, respectively. The letters in the pick patterns indicate which right-hand fingers play which strings.

p = thumb
i = index finger
m = middle finger
a = ring finger

For example; Pick Pattern 2
is played: thumb - index - middle - ring

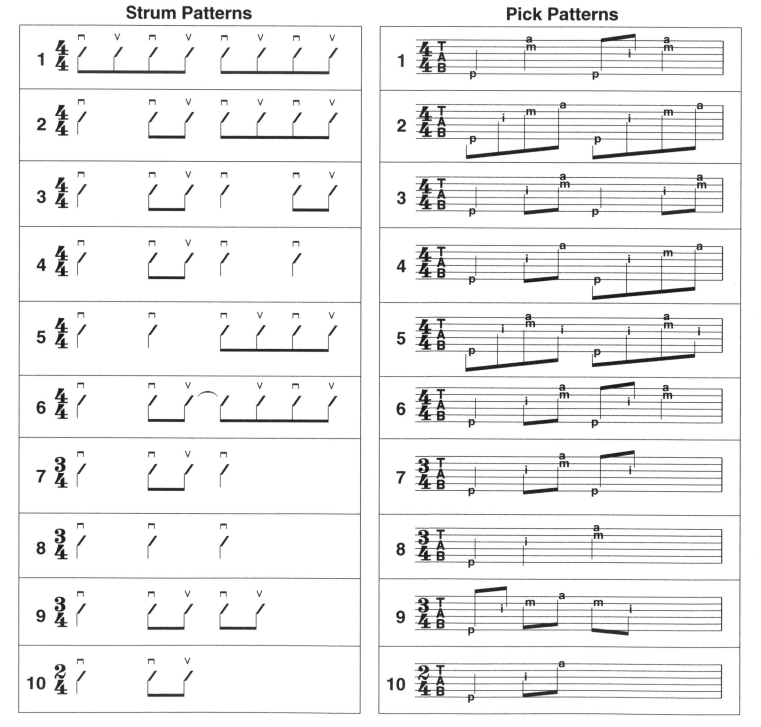

You can use the 3/4 Strum and Pick Patterns in songs written in compound meter (6/8, 9/8, 12/8, etc.). For example, you can accompany a song in 6/8 by playing the 3/4 pattern twice in each measure. The 4/4 Strum and Pick Patterns can be used for songs written in cut time (₵) by doubling the note time values in the patterns. Each pattern would therefore last two measures in cut time.

At the Hop

Words and Music by Arthur Singer, John Madara and David White

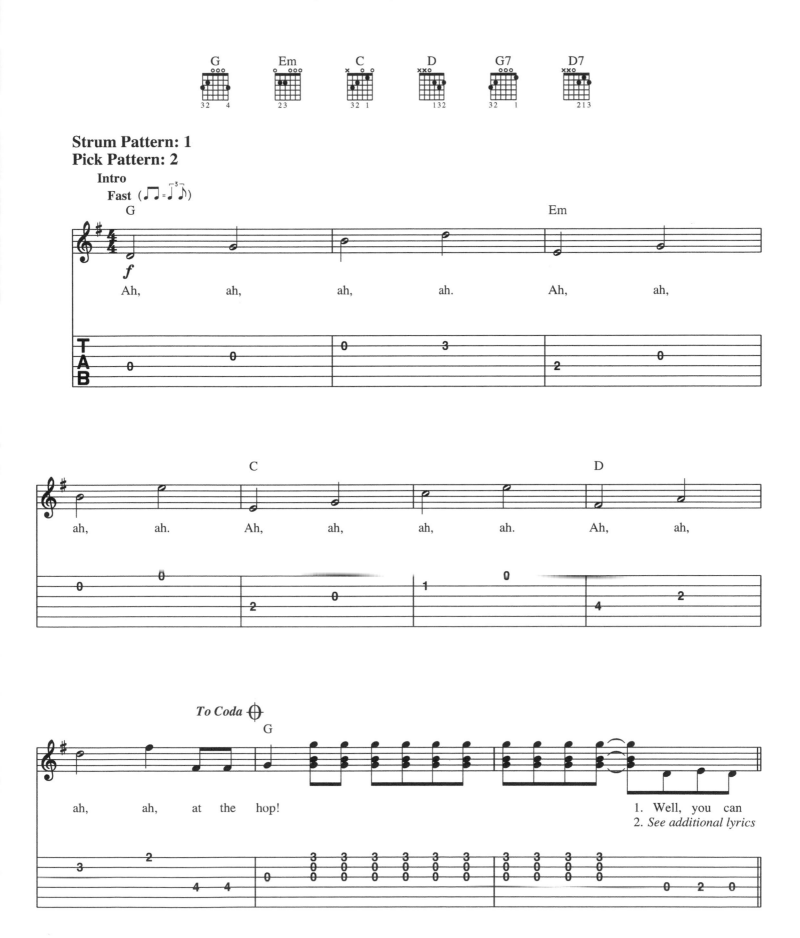

Verse

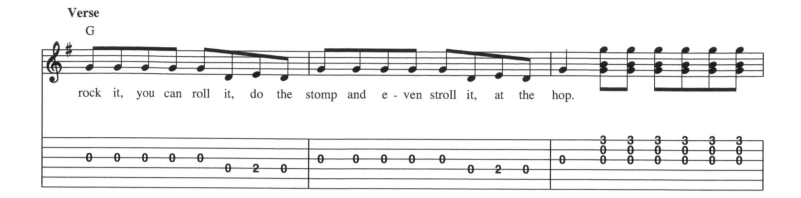

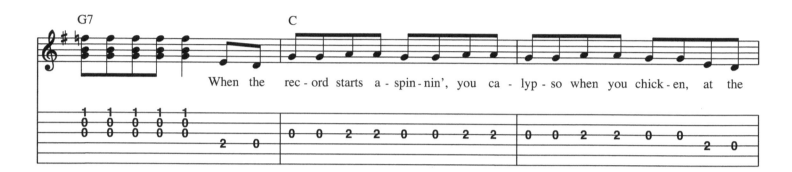

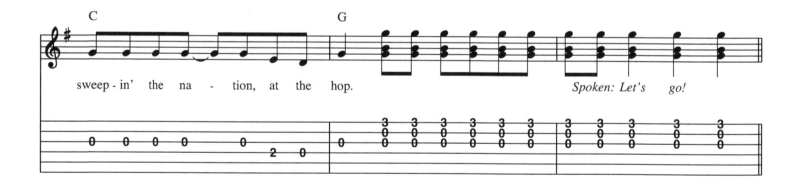

Chorus

(Oh, ba - by.) Let's go to the hop! (Oh, ba - by.)

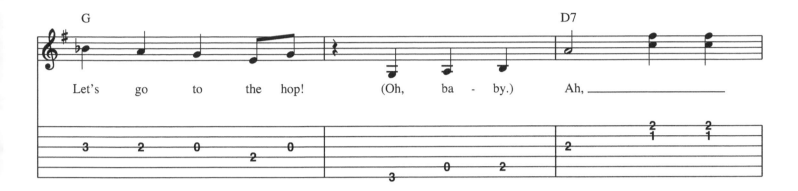

Let's go to the hop! (Oh, ba - by.) Ah, _____

ah, _____ let's go to the hop! 2. Well, you can

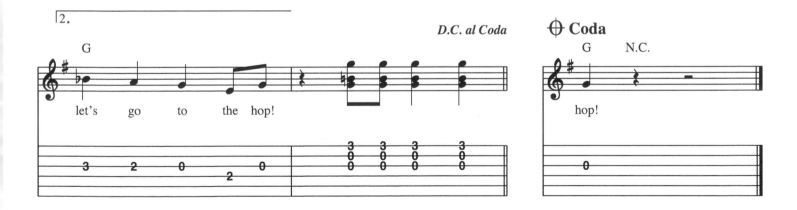

let's go to the hop! hop!

D.C. al Coda   ⊕ **Coda**

Additional Lyrics

2. Well, you can swing it, you can groove it,
   You can really start to move it, at the hop.
   Where the jumpin' is the smoothest
   And the music is the coolest, at the hop.
   All the cats and the chicks can get their kicks, at the hop.

All I Have to Do Is Dream

Words and Music by Boudleaux Bryant

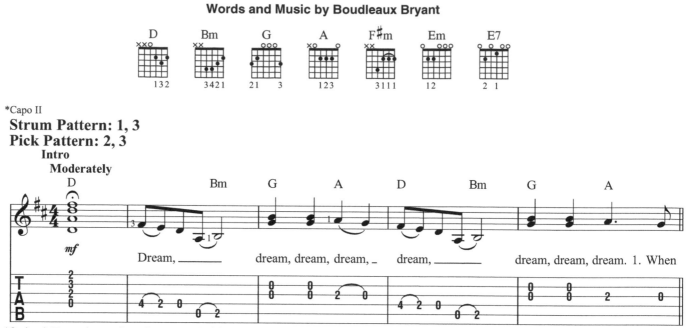

*Capo II
Strum Pattern: 1, 3
Pick Pattern: 2, 3
Intro
Moderately

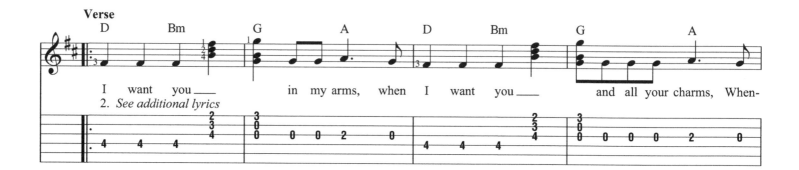

Dream, _____ dream, dream, dream, _ dream, _____ dream, dream, dream. 1. When

*Optional: To match recording, place capo at 2nd fret.

Verse

I want you _____ in my arms, when I want you _____ and all your charms, When-
2. *See additional lyrics*

ev - er I want you _ all I have to do is dream, _____ dream, dream, dream. 2. When

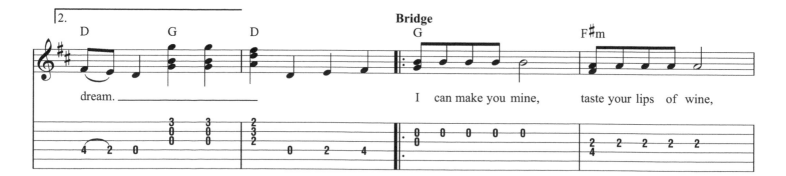

dream. _____ I can make you mine, taste your lips of wine,

an - y-time,   night or day.   On - ly trou-ble is,   gee _ whiz, I'm dream-ing my life _ a -

way!   3., 4. I   need you so ___   that I could die,   I love you so, ___   and that is why, when -

ev - er I want you ___   all I have to do   is dream, _____   dream, dream, dream, _

dream. _____   dream, dream, dream, _   dream, _____

Additional Lyrics

2. When I feel blue in the night
   And I need you to hold me tight,
   Whenever I want you
   All I have to do is dream.

Be-Bop-a-Lula

Words and Music by Tex Davis and Gene Vincent

Strum Pattern: 3
Pick Pattern: 3

loves me so, say, ___ Be-Bop-a-Lu - la, she's my ba - by. Be-Bop-a-Lu - la, I don't mean _ may - be.

2nd time, D.S. al Coda

Be-Bop-a-Lu - la, she's _____ my ba - by doll, my ba - by doll, my ba - by doll.

⊕ Coda

Chorus

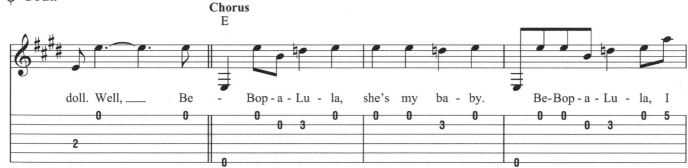

doll. Well, ___ Be - Bop-a-Lu - la, she's my ba - by. Be-Bop-a-Lu - la, I

don't mean _ may - be. Be-Bop-a-lu-la, she's my ba - by. Be-Bop-a-Lu - la, I don't mean _ may - be.

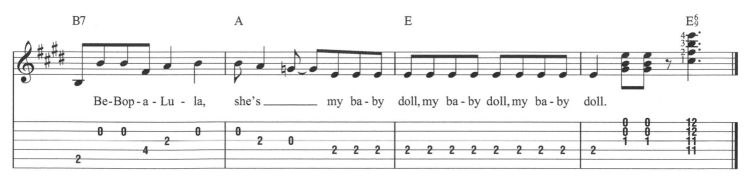

Be-Bop-a-Lu - la, she's _____ my ba - by doll, my ba - by doll, my ba - by doll.

Additional Lyrics

2. Well, now she's the woman that's got that beat,
Oh, she's the woman with the flyin' feet.
Ah she's the woman that walks around the store,
She's the woman that yells more, more, more, more.

Bird Dog

Words and Music by Boudleaux Bryant

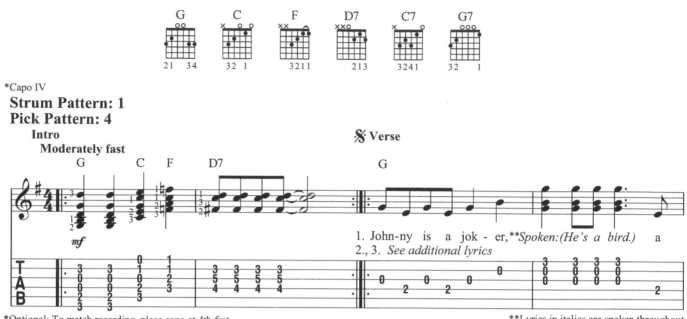

*Capo IV

Strum Pattern: 1
Pick Pattern: 4

Intro
Moderately fast

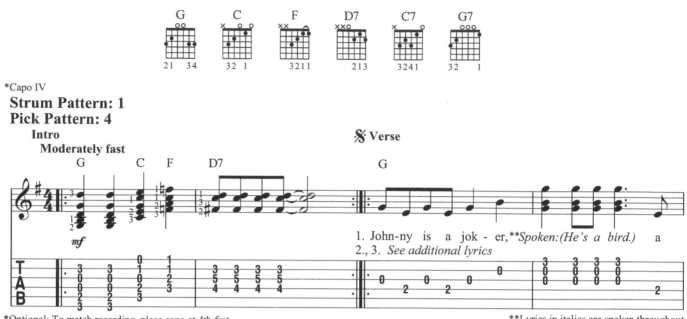

1. John-ny is a jok - er,**Spoken:*(He's a bird.)* a
2., 3. *See additional lyrics*

*Optional: To match recording, place capo at 4th fret.

**Lyrics in italics are spoken throughout.

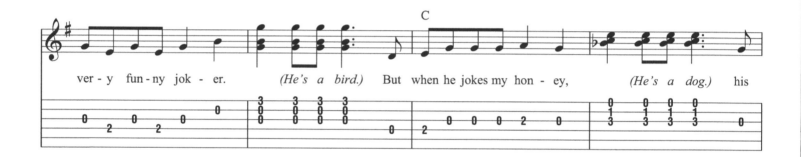

ver - y fun - ny jok - er. *(He's a bird.)* But when he jokes my hon - ey, *(He's a dog.)* his

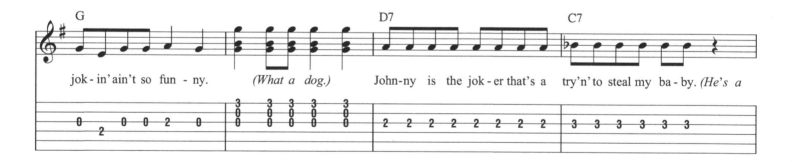

jok - in' ain't so fun - ny. *(What a dog.)* John-ny is the jok - er that's a try'n' to steal my ba - by. *(He's a*

bird dog.) Hey, bird dog, get a - way from my quail. _

Hey, bird dog, you're on ___ the wrong trail. Bird dog, you'd bet-ter leave my lov-ey dove ___ a - lone.

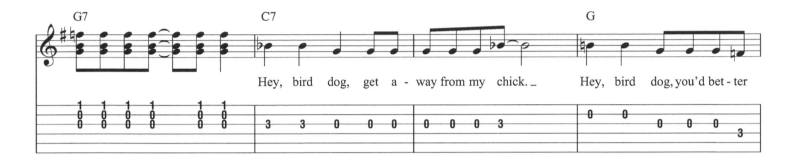

Hey, bird dog, get a - way from my chick. ___ Hey, bird dog, you'd bet - ter

get a - way quick. ___ Bird dog, you'd bet - ter find a chick-en lit - tle of your own.

⊕ Coda

To Coda ⊕   *D.S. al Coda (no repeat)*   *Repeat and fade*

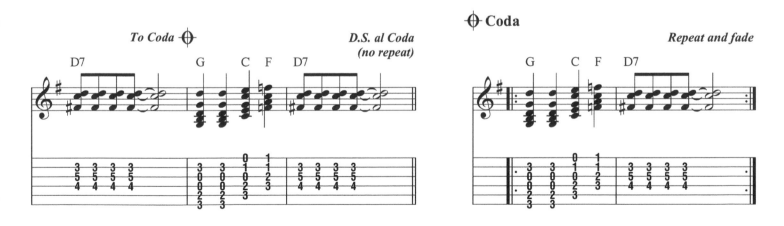

Additional Lyrics

2. Johnny sings a love song, *(Like a bird.)*
   He sings the sweetest love song. *(You ever heard.)*
   But when he sings to my gal, *(What a howl.)*
   To me he's just a wolf dog. *(On the prowl.)*
   Johnny wants to fly away and puppy love my baby.
   (He's a bird dog.)

3. Johnny kissed the teacher; *(He's a bird.)*
   He tiptoed up to reach her. *(He's a bird.)*
   Well, he's the teacher's pet now; *(He's a dog.)*
   What he wants he can get now. *(What a dog.)*
   He even made the teacher let him sit next to my baby.
   (He's a bird dog.)

Blue Suede Shoes

Words and Music by Carl Lee Perkins

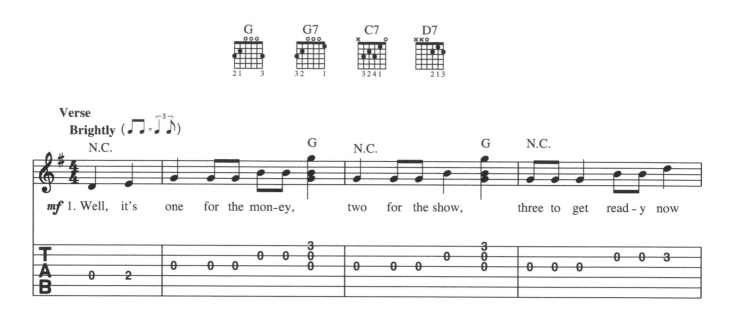

Verse
Brightly

N.C.
1. Well, it's one for the mon-ey, two for the show, three to get read-y now

Strum Pattern: 2, 3
Pick Pattern: 3, 4

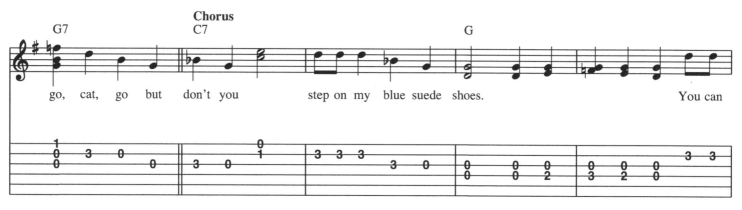

Chorus
go, cat, go but don't you step on my blue suede shoes. You can

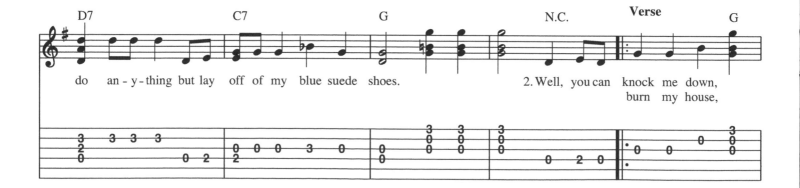

do an-y-thing but lay off of my blue suede shoes. 2. Well, you can knock me down, burn my house,

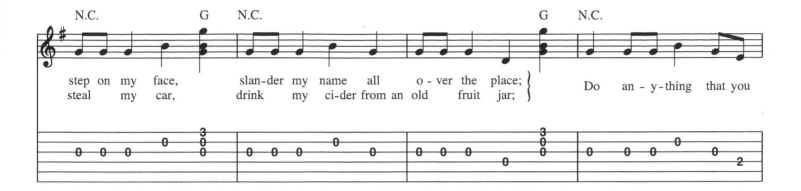

step on my face, slan-der my name all o-ver the place; Do an-y-thing that you
steal my car, drink my ci-der from an old fruit jar;

want to do but uh-huh, hon-ey, lay off of my shoes. Now don't you

Chorus

step on my blue suede shoes. You can do an-y-thing but lay

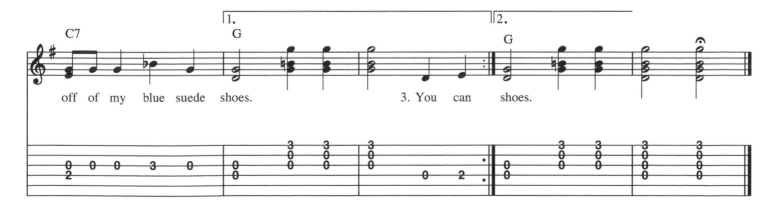

off of my blue suede shoes. 3. You can shoes.

Bluejean Bop

Words and Music by Gene Vincent and Hal Levy

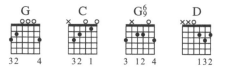

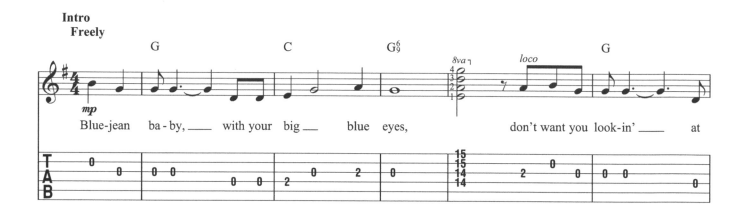

Strum Pattern: 3
Pick Pattern: 3

Verse

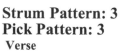

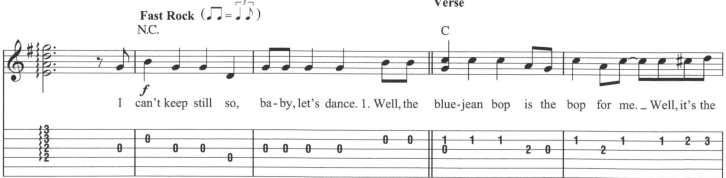

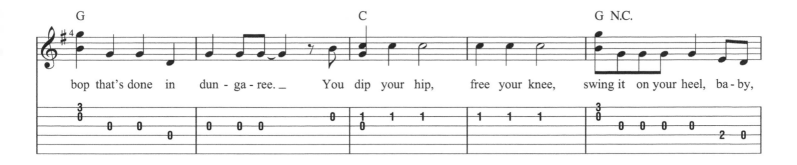

bop that's done in dun - ga - ree. __ You dip your hip, free your knee, swing it on your heel, ba - by,

𝄋 Chorus

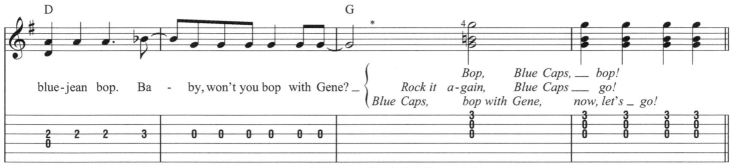

one, two, three. Well, the blue - jean bop, blue - jean bop, oh, ba - by, blue - jean bop, blue - jean bop, oh, ba - by,

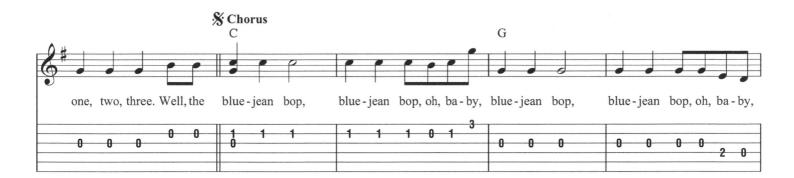

blue - jean bop. Ba - by, won't you bop with Gene? __

Bop, Blue Caps, __ bop!
Rock it a - gain, Blue Caps __ go!
Blue Caps, bop with Gene, now, let's __ go!

*Lyrics in italics are spoken.

Instrumental

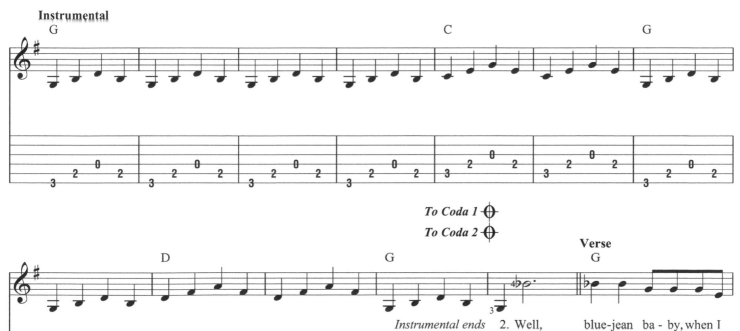

To Coda 1 ⊕
To Coda 2 ⊕

Verse

Instrumental ends 2. Well, blue - jean ba - by, when I

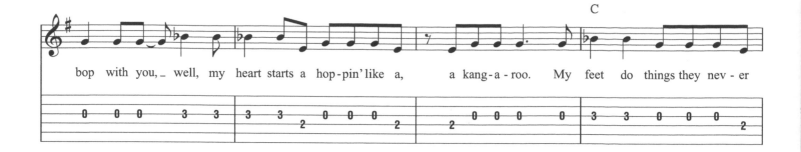

bop with you, _ well, my heart starts a hop-pin' like a, a kang-a-roo. My feet do things they nev - er

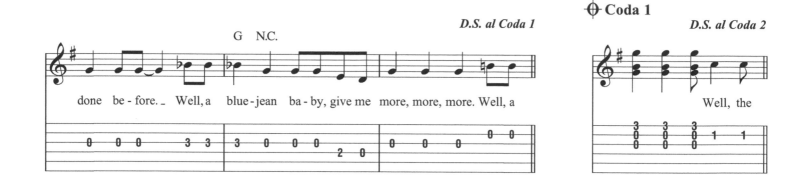

D.S. al Coda 1

Coda 1

D.S. al Coda 2

done be - fore. _ Well, a blue-jean ba - by, give me more, more, more. Well, a

Well, the

Coda 2

Outro

Well, it's a blue - jean, a blue-jean bop. A blue - jean, a

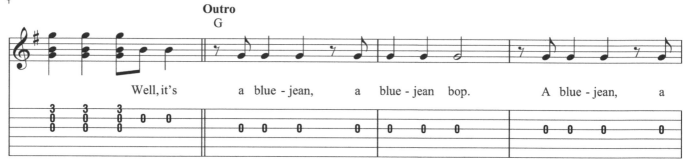

blue-jean bop, oh, ba-by, a blue-jean, a blue-jean bop. A blue-jean, a blue-jean bop.

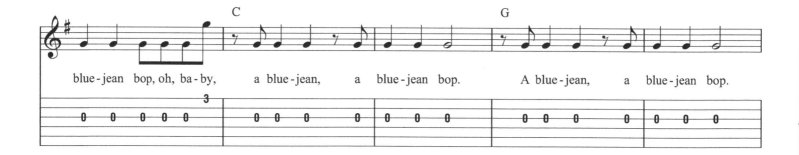

A blue-jean, oh ba-by won't you bop with Gene? _

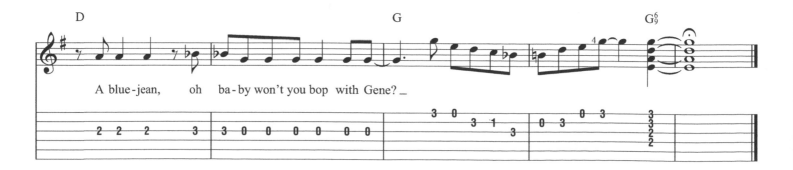

Bo Diddley

Words and Music by Ellas McDaniel

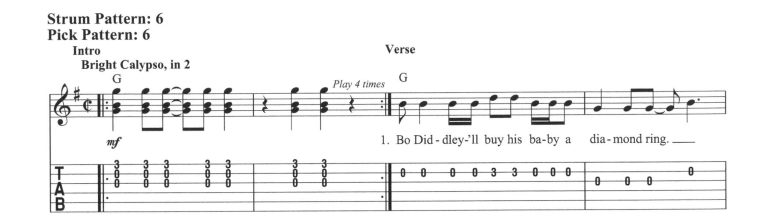

Strum Pattern: 6
Pick Pattern: 6

Intro

Verse

Bright Calypso, in 2

Play 4 times

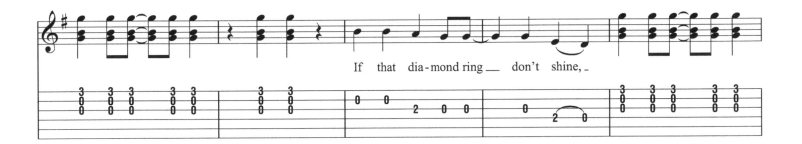

1. Bo Did-dley-'ll buy his ba-by a dia-mond ring. ___

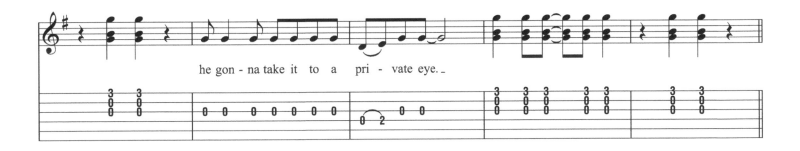

If that dia-mond ring ___ don't shine, _

he gon-na take it to a pri-vate eye. _

Verse

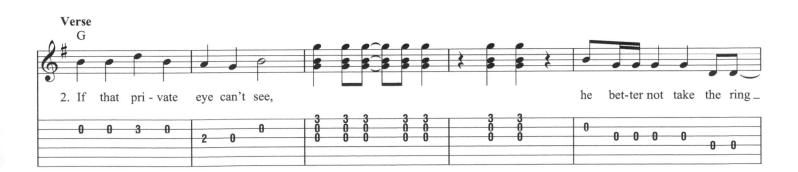

2. If that pri-vate eye can't see,   he bet-ter not take the ring ___

from me.

Verse

3. Bo Did-dley caught a nan - ny goat ____
4. Bo Did-dley caught a bear - cat __

to make his pret-ty ba-by a Sun - day coat. __
to make his pret-ty ba-by a Sun - day hat. __

Guitar Solo

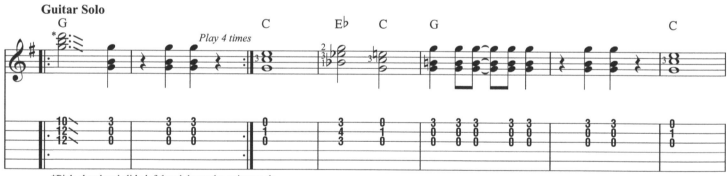

*Pick chord and slide left hand down the guitar neck.

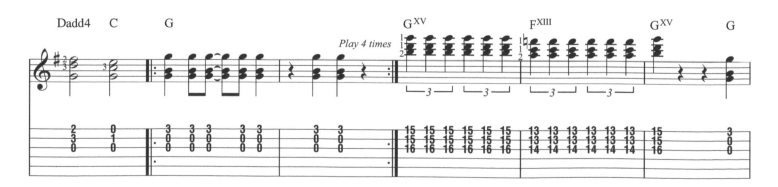

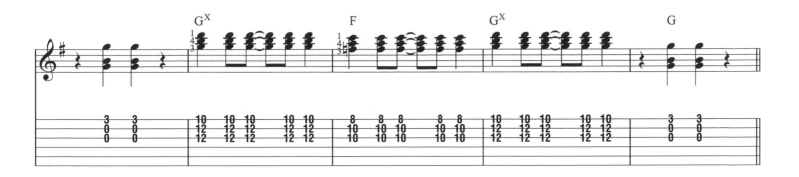

Verse
G

5. Won't you come to my house and rack that bone?
6. Look at that bo - do, oh, where's he been?

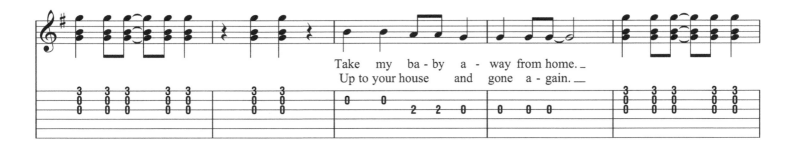

Take my ba - by a - way from home.
Up to your house and gone a - gain.

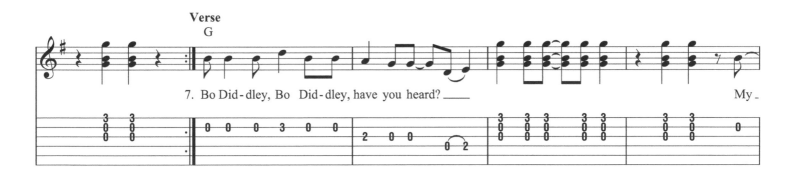

Verse
G

7. Bo Did - dley, Bo Did - dley, have you heard?   My

Outro

Repeat and fade

G

— pret - ty ba - by said she was a bird.

Book of Love

Words and Music by Warren Davis, George Malone and Charles Patrick

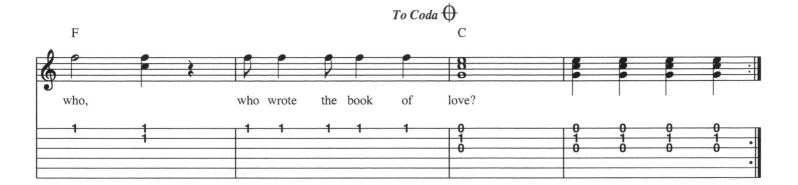

To Coda ⊕

who,   who wrote the book of love?

Bridge

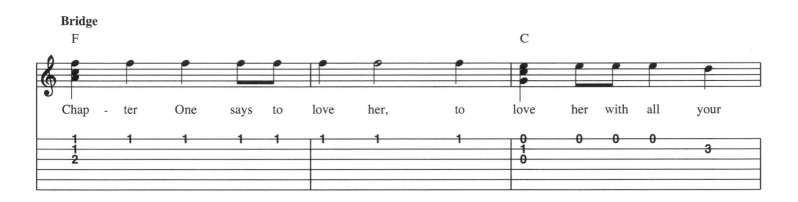

Chap - ter One says to love her,   to love her with all your

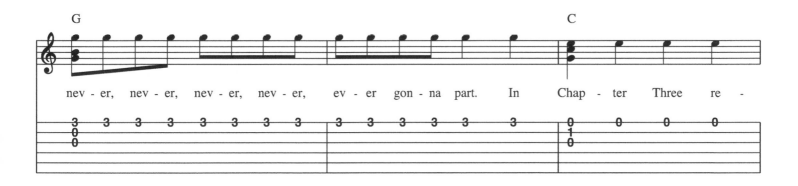

heart.   Chap - ter Two you tell her, you're

never, nev - er, nev - er, nev - er, ev - er gon - na part. In Chap - ter Three re -

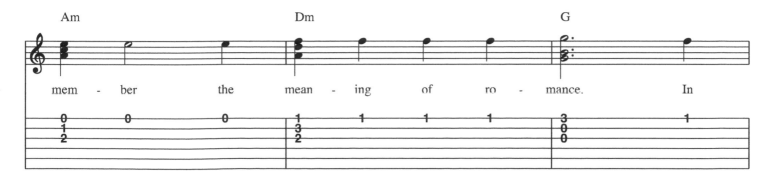

mem - ber the mean - ing of ro - mance. In

Chap - ter Four you break up, but you give her just one more

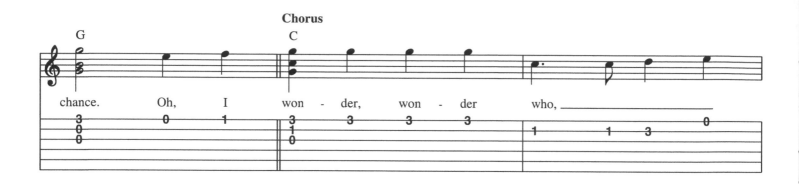

Chorus

chance. Oh, I won - der, won - der who,

D.S. al Coda

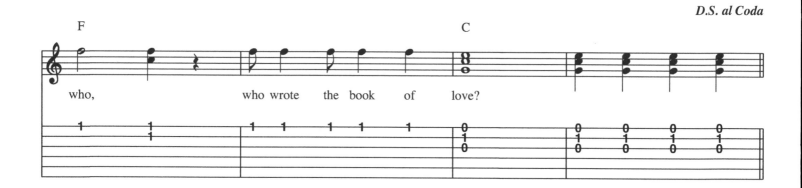

who, who wrote the book of love?

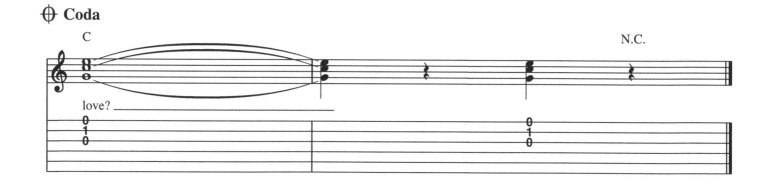

⊕ Coda

love?

N.C.

Additional Lyrics

2. I love you, darling,
   Baby, you know I do.
   But I've got to see this book of love,
   Find out why it's true.

3. Baby, baby, baby,
   I love you, yes, I do.
   Well, it says so in this book of love,
   Ours is the one that's true.

Charlie Brown

Words and Music by Jerry Leiber and Mike Stoller

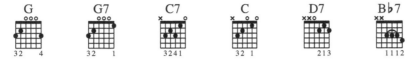

Strum Pattern: 4
Pick Pattern: 3

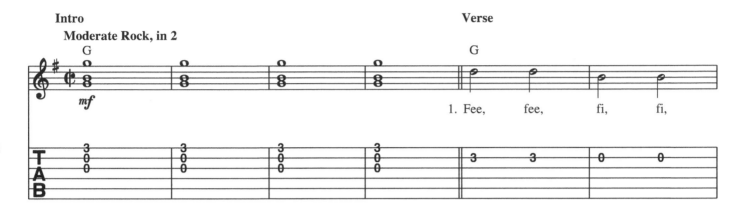

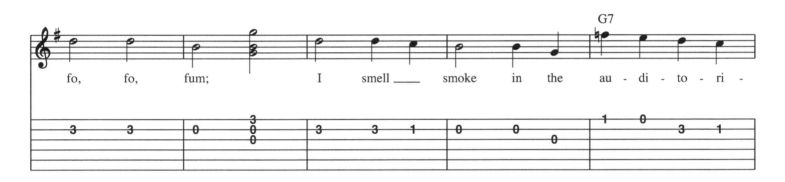

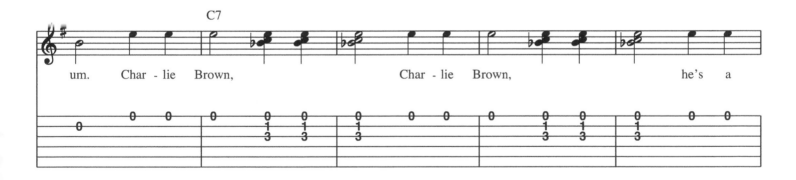

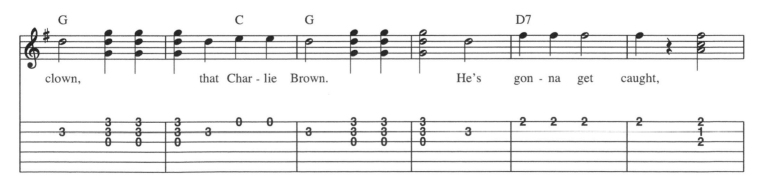

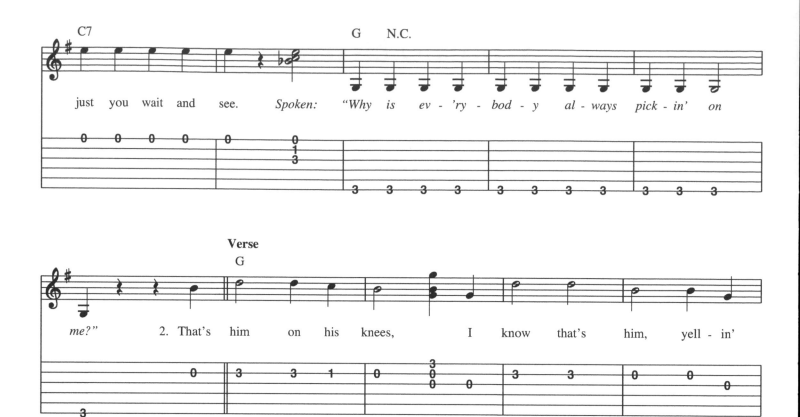

just you wait and see. *Spoken:* *"Why is ev - 'ry - bod - y al - ways pick - in' on*

Verse

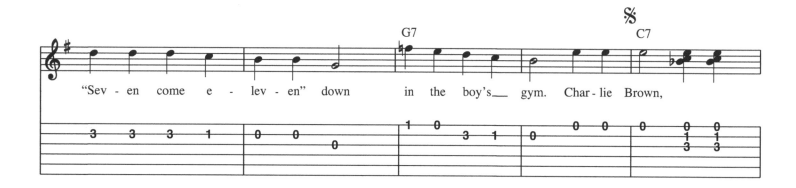

me?" 2. That's him on his knees, I know that's him, yell - in'

"Sev - en come e - lev - en" down in the boy's___ gym. Char - lie Brown,

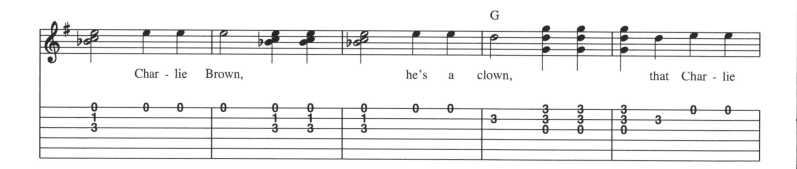

Char - lie Brown, he's a clown, that Char - lie

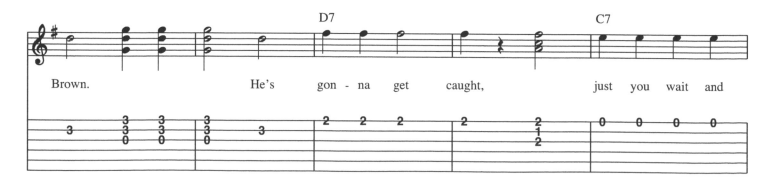

Brown. He's gon - na get caught, just you wait and

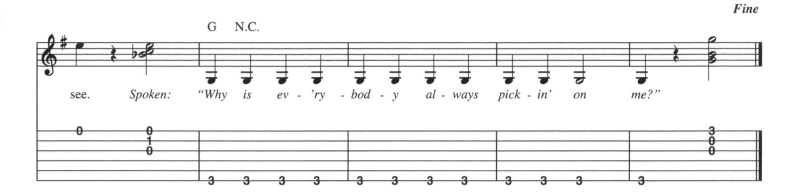

see. *Spoken:* "Why is ev - 'ry - bod - y al - ways pick - in' on me?"

Bridge

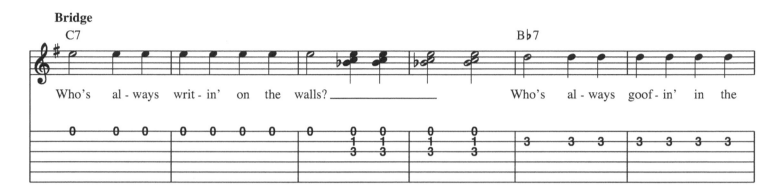

Who's al - ways writ - in' on the walls? _____ Who's al - ways goof - in' in the

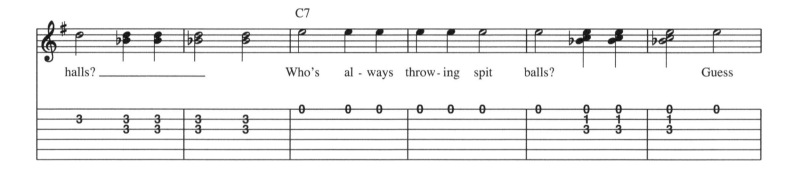

halls? _____ Who's al - ways throw - ing spit balls? Guess

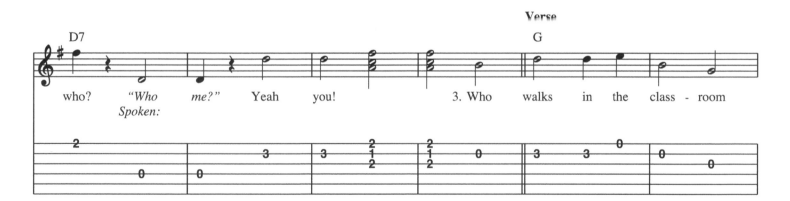

who? *"Who me?"* Yeah you! 3. Who walks in the class - room
Spoken:

D.S. al Fine

cool and slow? Who calls the Eng - lish teach - er "dad - dy - o?" Char - lie

Boppin' the Blues

Words and Music by Carl Lee Perkins and Howard Griffin

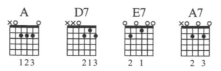

Strum Pattern: 3, 4
Pick Pattern: 4, 5

Chorus
Moderately fast

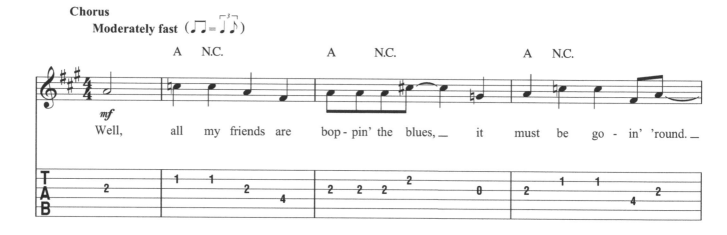

Well, all my friends are bop-pin' the blues, __ it must be go - in' 'round. __

__ All __ my friends are bop - pin' the blues, __ it

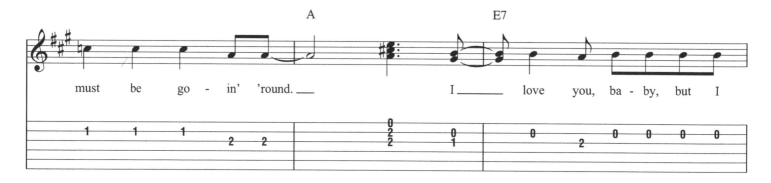

must be go - in' 'round. __ I __ love you, ba - by, but I

must be ___ rhy - thm bound. __ 1. Well, __ the

Verse

doc - tor told __ me, "Carl, __ you don't need no pills." Hey, __ the

2. *See additional lyrics*
3. *Instrumental*

doc - tor told __ me, "Boy, __ you don't need no pills, just a

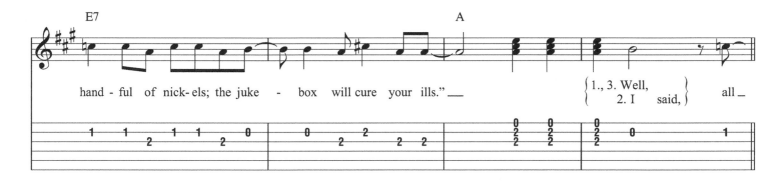

hand - ful of nick - els; the juke - box will cure your ills." __ { 1., 3. Well, / 2. I said, } all __

𝄋 Chorus

__ my friends are bop - pin' the blues, __ it must be go - in' 'round. __ All __

{ 1., 3. them cats just / 2., 4. my friends are } bop - pin' the blues __ and it must be go - in' 'round. __ I __

To Coda ⊕

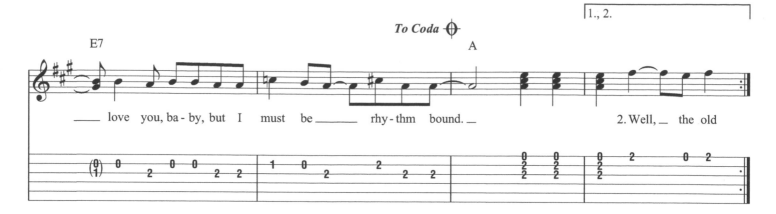

— love you, ba - by, but I must be _____ rhy - thm bound. —   2. Well, — the old

3.

Verse

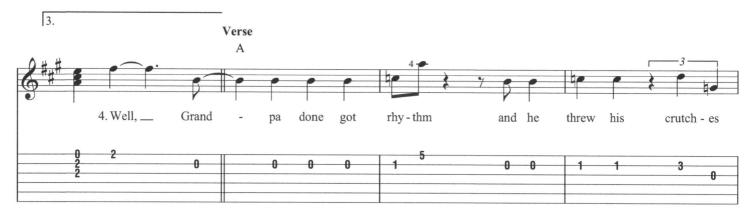

4. Well, — Grand - pa done got rhy - thm   and he threw his crutch - es

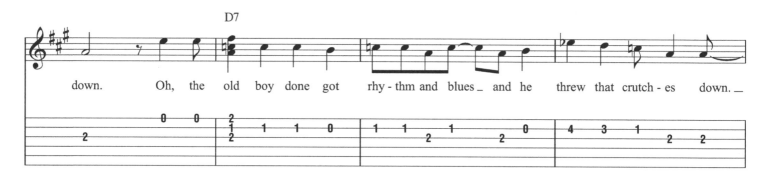

down.   Oh, the old boy done got rhy - thm and blues — and he threw that crutch - es   down. —

—   Grand - ma, he ain't — tri - flin',   well, the old boy's ____ rhy - thm bound. —

D.S. al Coda   ⊕ **Coda**

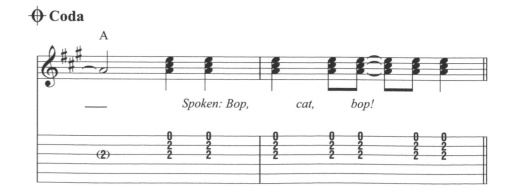

—   All —   —   *Spoken: Bop,*   *cat,*   *bop!*

Outro

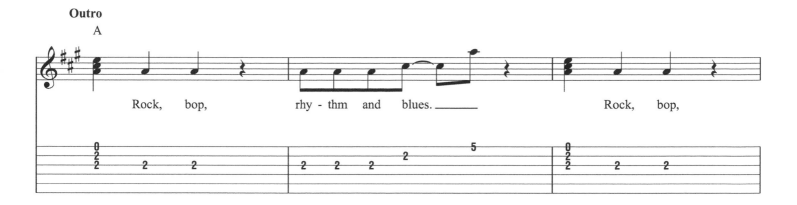

Rock, bop, rhy - thm and blues. _____ Rock, bop,

rhy - thm and blues. _ Rock, bop, rhy - thm and blues. _

Rock, bop, rhy - thm and blues. _ Rhy - thm and blues, _ it

must be _ go - in' 'round. _

Additional Lyrics

2. Well, the old cat bug bit me,
   Man, I don't feel no pain.
   Yeah, that jitterbug caught me,
   Man, I don't feel no pain.
   I still love you, baby,
   But I'll never be the same.

Bye Bye Love

Words and Music by Felice Bryant and Boudleaux Bryant

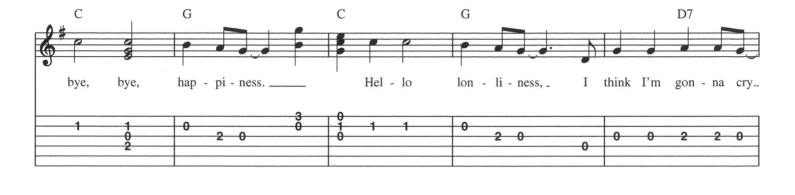

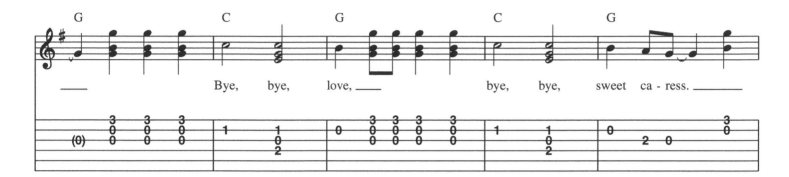

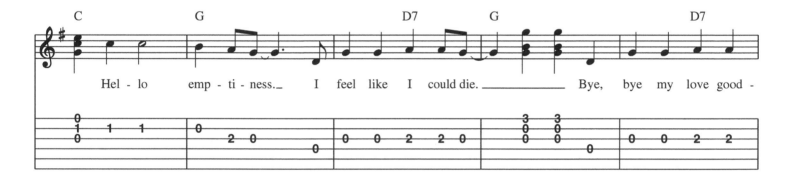

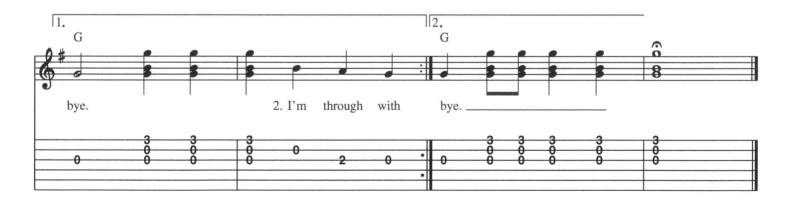

Additional Lyrics

2. I'm through with romance, I'm through with love.
   I'm through with counting the stars above.
   And here's the reason that I'm so free,
   My lovin' baby is through with me.

Down the Road a Piece

Words and Music by Don Raye

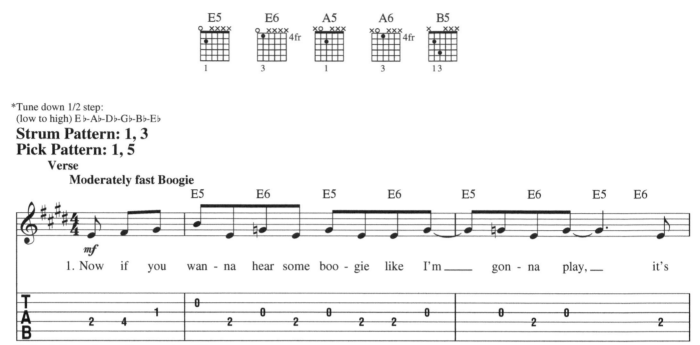

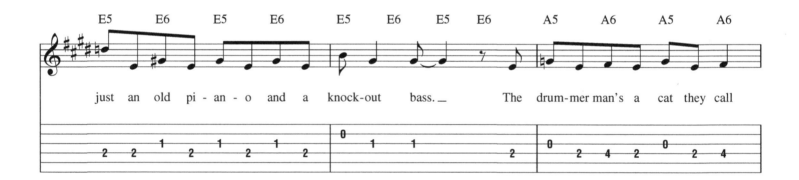

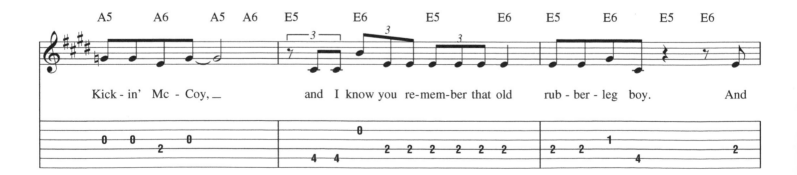

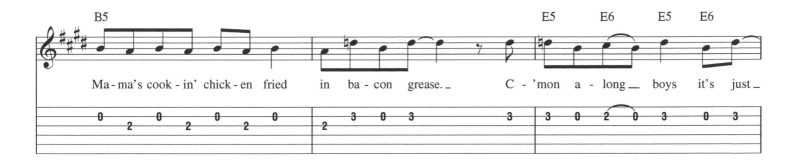

Ma-ma's cook-in' chick-en fried in ba-con grease._ C-'mon a-long_ boys it's just_

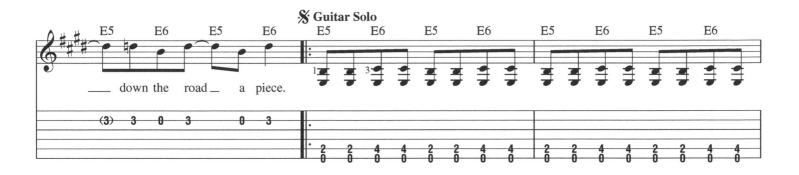

% Guitar Solo

_ down the road _ a piece.

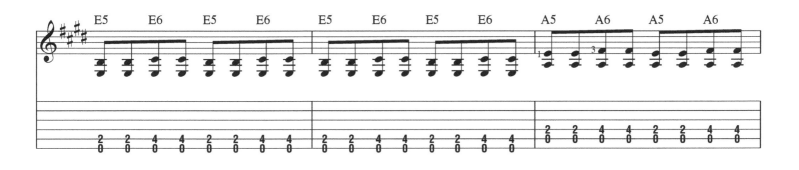

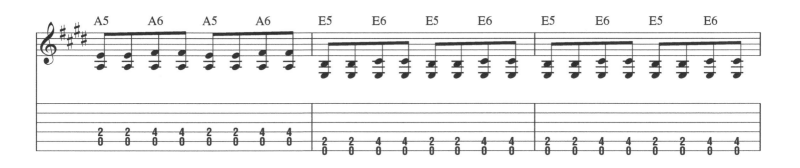

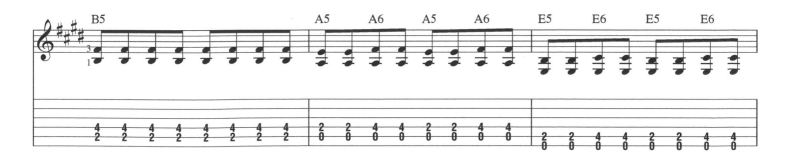

2. Now there's ___
3. There's } a place you'll real - ly get your kicks, ___ it's

o - pen ev - 'ry night from 'bout twelve to six. ___ And if you wan - na get some boo - gie you can

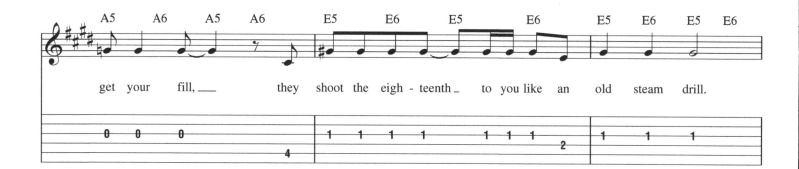

get your fill, ___ they shoot the eigh - teenth ___ to you like an old steam drill.

2nd time, D.S. and fade

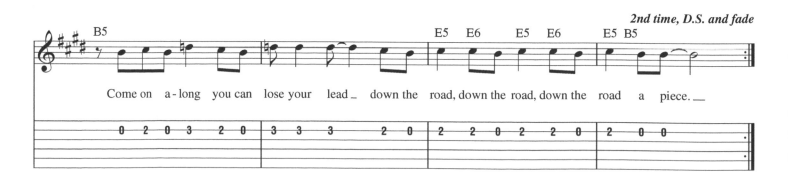

Come on a - long you can lose your lead ___ down the road, down the road, down the road a piece. ___

34

Earth Angel

Words and Music by Jesse Belvin

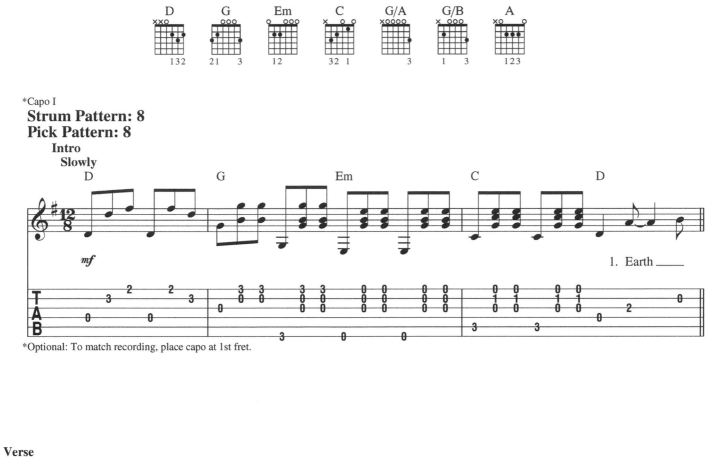

*Optional: To match recording, place capo at 1st fret.

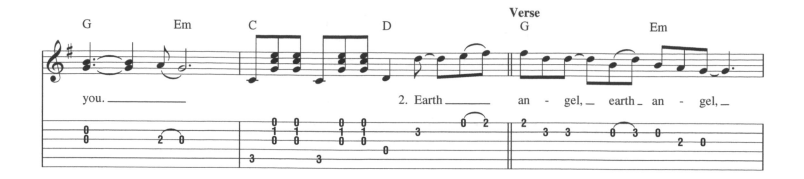

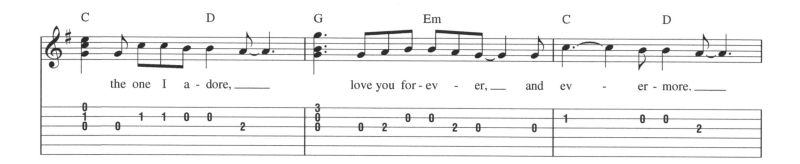

vi - sion __ of your hap, __ hap-pi - ness. 3., 4. Oh, _____ oh, __ earth an - gel, __ earth __ an - gel, __

please __ be mine. _____ My dar - ling, dear, _____ love you __ all the time. _____

I'm just a fool, _____ a __ fool in love with you. _____ I

I'm just a fool, _____ a fool in love __ with __ you. _____
(You, you, you.)
let ring - - - - - - - - - - - - - - -

*Let chord ring.

Good Golly Miss Molly

Words and Music by Robert Blackwell and John Marascalco

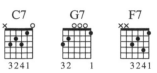

Strum Pattern: 1, 2
Pick Pattern: 2, 4

call? 1. From the ear - ly, ear - ly morn - in' to the
2., 3. *See additional lyrics*

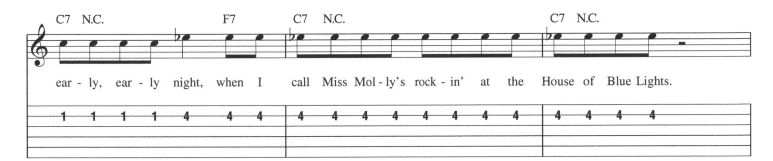

ear - ly, ear - ly night, when I call Miss Mol - ly's rock - in' at the House of Blue Lights.

Chorus

Good gol - ly Miss Mol - ly sure ___ likes to ball. ___

When you're rock - in' and a rol - lin', can't you hear ___ your ma - ma

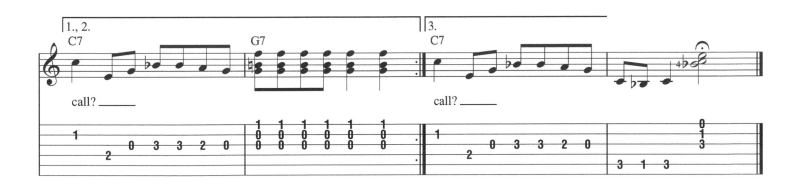

call? ___ call? ___

Additional Lyrics

2. Mama, Poppa told me, "Son,
 You better watch your step.
 If they knew about Miss Molly
 Have to watch my pop myself."

3. Going to the corner,
 Gonna buy a diamond ring.
 When she hugs and kisses me,
 Makes me ting a ling a ling.

Great Balls of Fire

Words and Music by Otis Blackwell and Jack Hammer

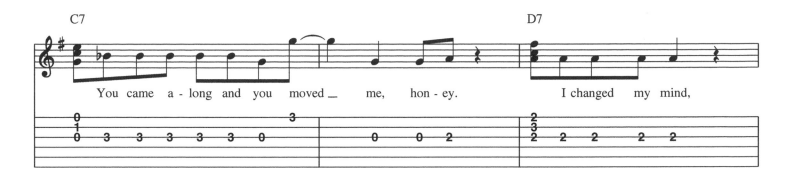

You came a-long and you moved __ me, hon - ey. I changed my mind,

love's just fine. __ Good - ness gra - cious, great __ balls of fire!
Instrumental ends

Bridge

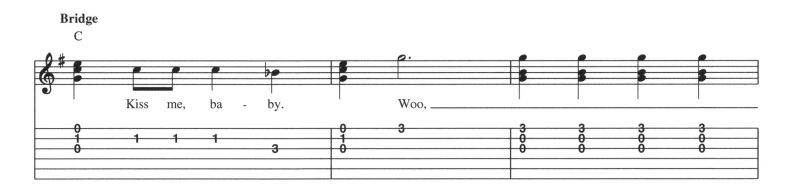

Kiss me, ba - by. Woo, __

__ it feels good. Hold me, ba - by.

Girl, just let me love you like a lov - er should. __ }
I want to love you like a lov - er should. __ }
You're fine, __

so kind, __ I'm gon-na tell the world that you're mine, mine, mine, mine. __

Outro

I chew my nails and I twid-dle my thumb. __ I'm real ner-vous but it

sure is fun. __ Come on, ba-by, you're driv-ing me cra-zy.

1.

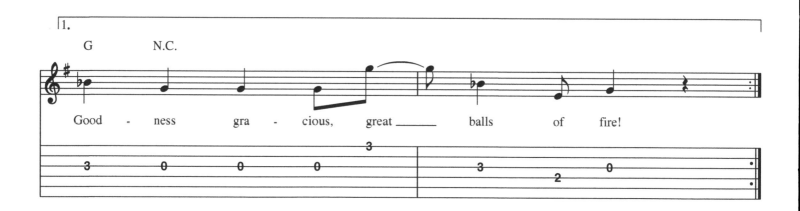

Good - ness gra - cious, great _____ balls of fire!

2.

Good - ness gra - cious, great _____ balls of fire!

I'm a Man

Words and Music by Ellas McDaniel

*Capo III

Strum Pattern: 1
Pick Pattern: 4

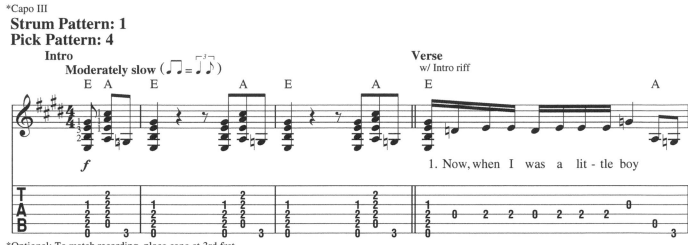

*Optional: To match recording, place capo at 3rd fret.

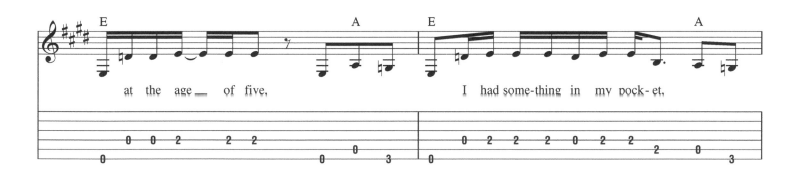

You know, ba - by, we can have a lot of fun. I'm a man.

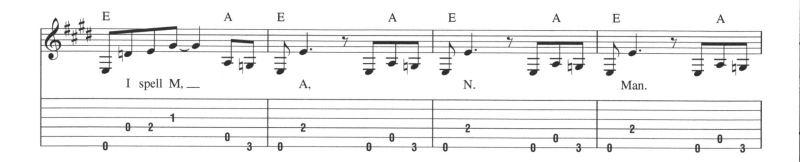

I spell M, __ A, N. Man.

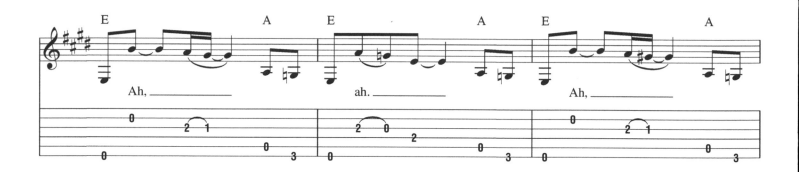

Ah, _____ ah. _____ Ah, _____

Verse
w/ Intro riff

ah. _____ 2. All you pret-ty wom-en __ stand in line, __
4. *See additional lyrics*

I can make love to you, ba-by, in an ho-ur's time. _ I'm a man.

Spelled M,   A,   N.   Man.

D.S. al Coda

Harmonica Solo

Play 3 times

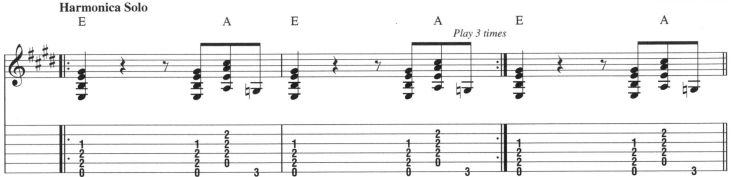

⊕ Coda

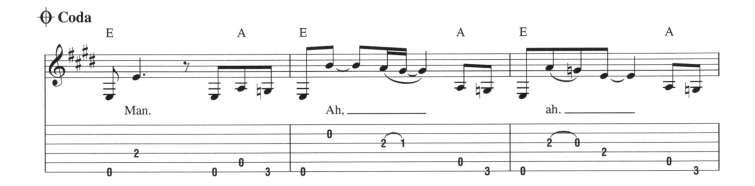

Man.   Ah, _____   ah. _____

Ah, _____   ah. _____   Oh.

Additional Lyrics

3. I'm goin' back down
   To Kansas soon.
   Bring back a second cousin,
   Little John the Conqueroo.
   I'm a man.
   Spelled M, A, N.
   Man.
   Ah, ah. Ah, ah.

4. The line I shoot
   Will never miss.
   The way I make love to 'em,
   They came for this.
   I'm a man.
   Spelled M, A, N.
   Man.
   Ah, ah. Ah, ah. Oh.

The Great Pretender

Words and Music by Buck Ram

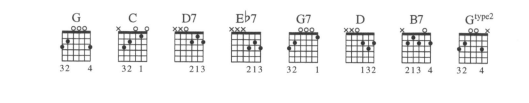

Strum Pattern: 8
Pick Pattern: 8

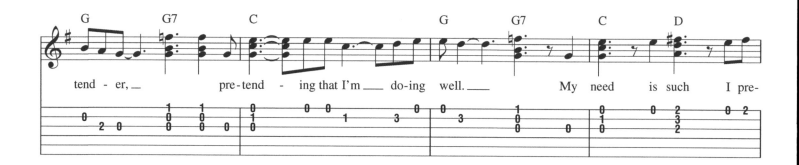

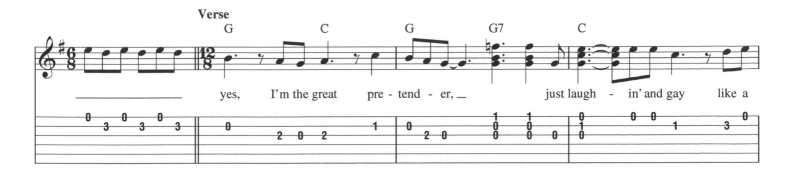

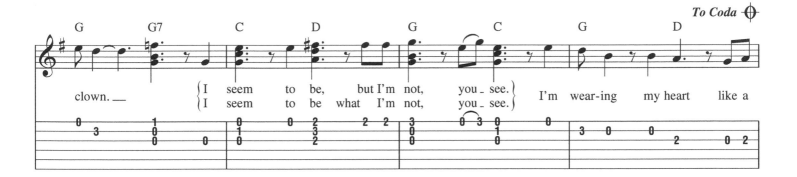

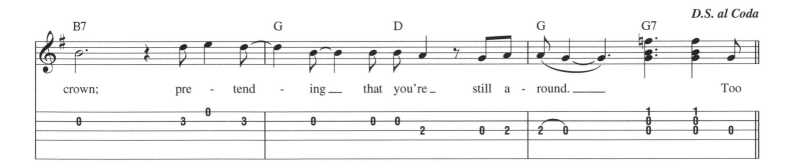

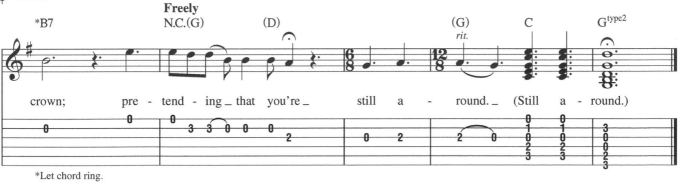

*Let chord ring.

Additional Lyrics

2. Oh, yes, I'm the great pretender,
Adrift in a world of my own.
I play the game, but to my real shame,
You've left me to dream all alone.

Guitar Boogie Shuffle

By Arthur Smith

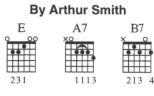

E   A7   B7

Strum Pattern: 3, 4
Pick Pattern: 3, 4

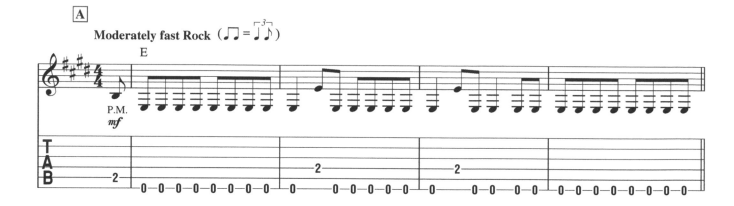

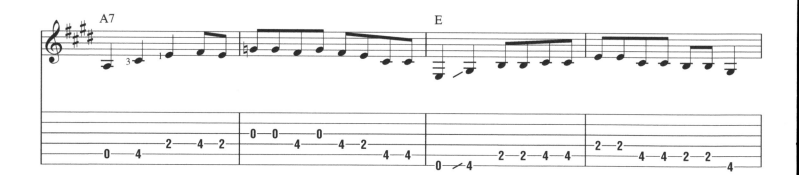

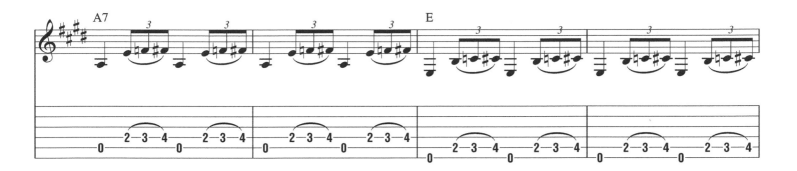

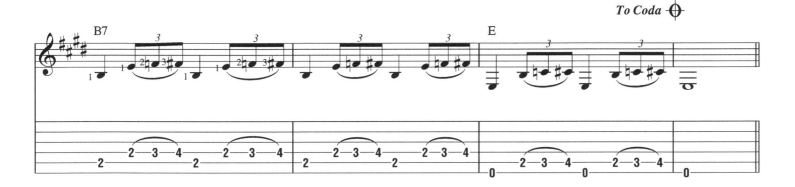

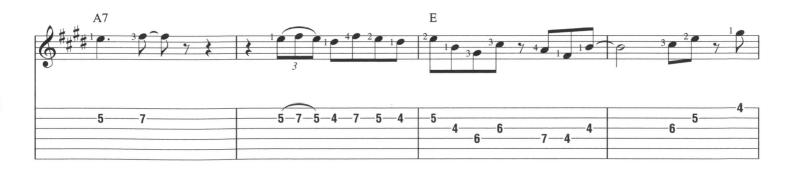

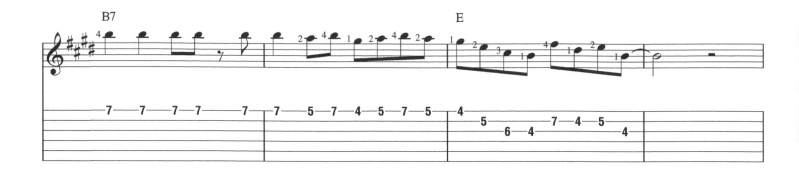

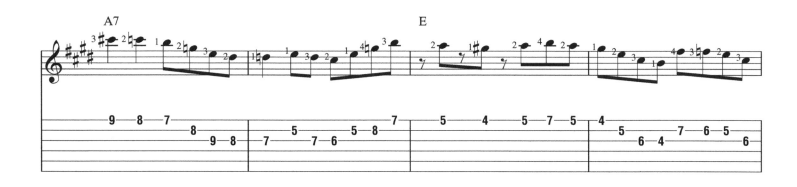

D.S. al Coda

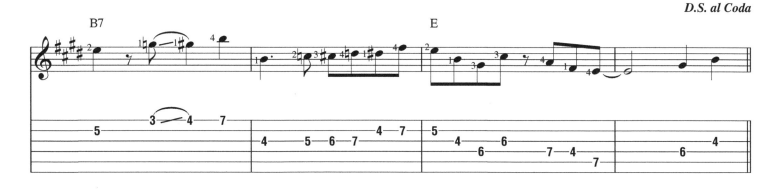

 Coda

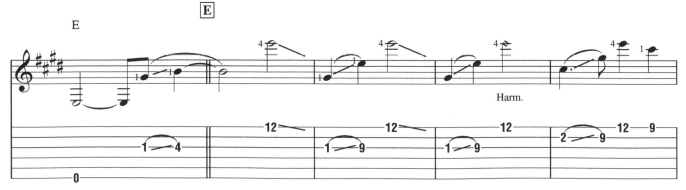

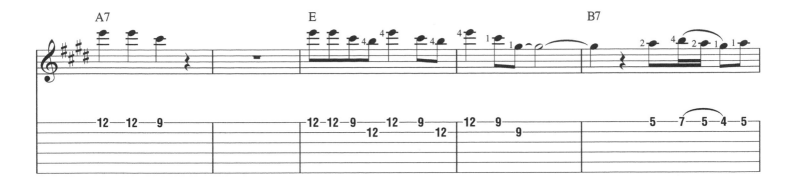

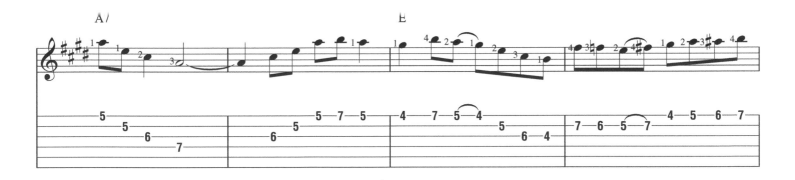

D.S.S. and fade
(take repeat)

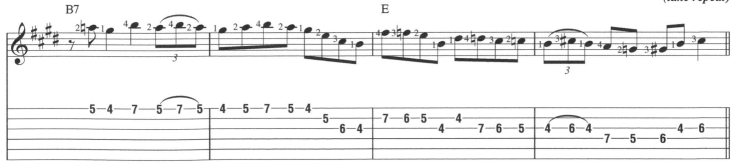

Honky Tonk (Parts 1 & 2)

Words and Music by Berisford "Shep" Shepherd, Clifford Scott, Bill Doggett and Billy Butler

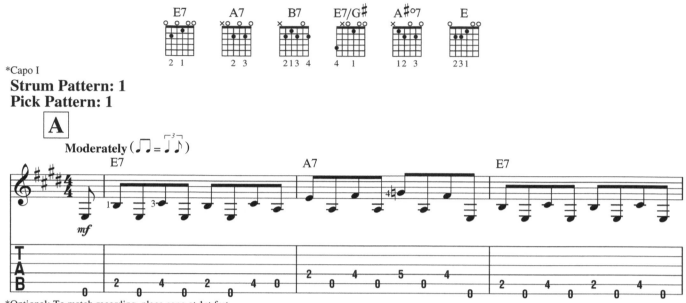

*Capo I

Strum Pattern: 1
Pick Pattern: 1

*Optional: To match recording, place capo at 1st fret.

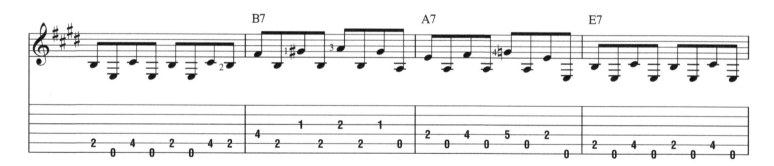

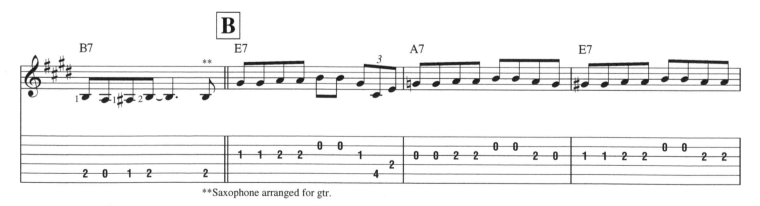

**Saxophone arranged for gtr.

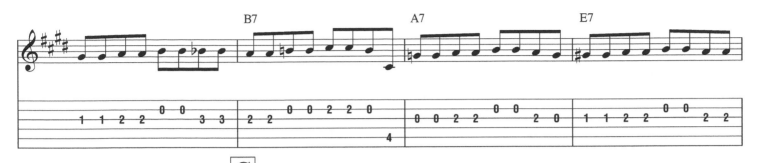

C

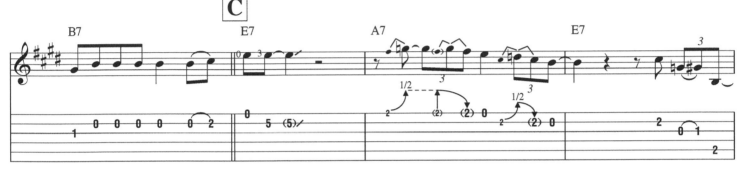

D

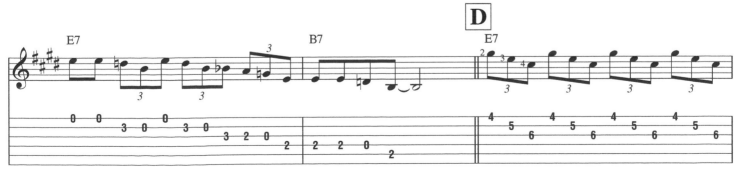

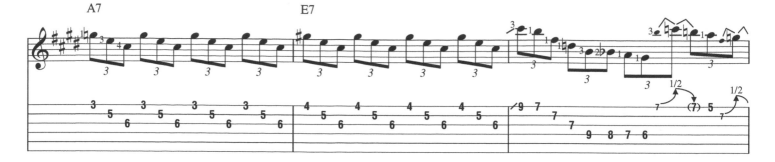

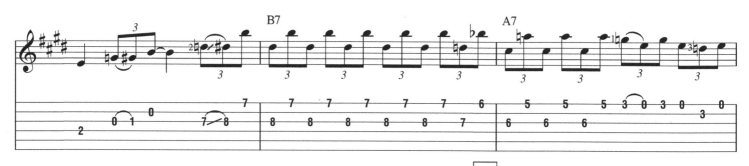

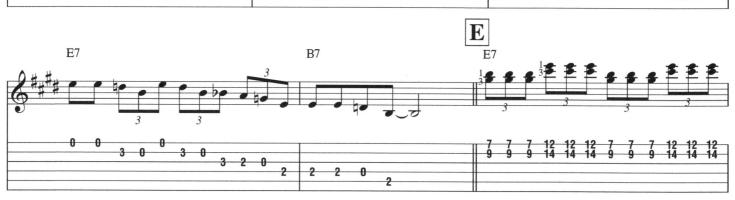

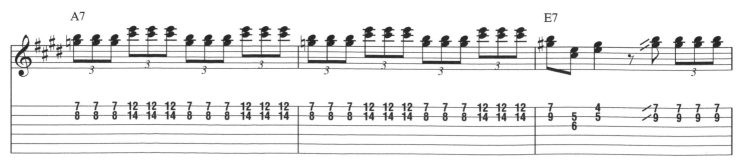

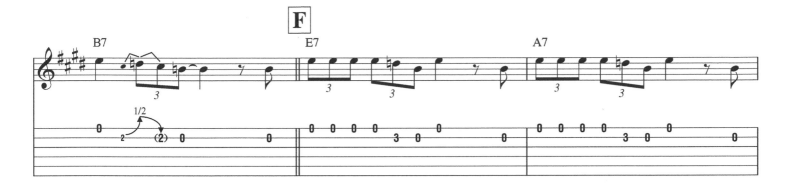

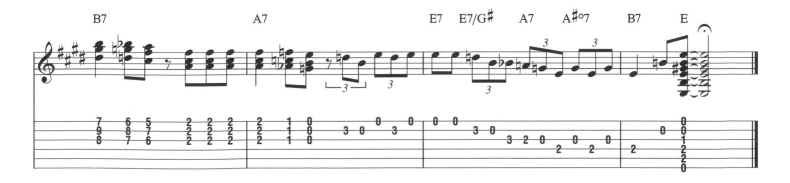

Hound Dog

Words and Music by Jerry Leiber and Mike Stoller

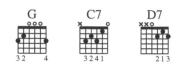

Strum Pattern: 2, 5
Pick Pattern: 4

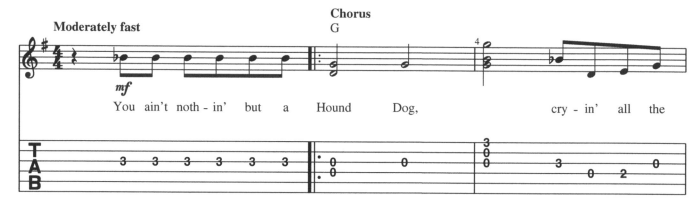

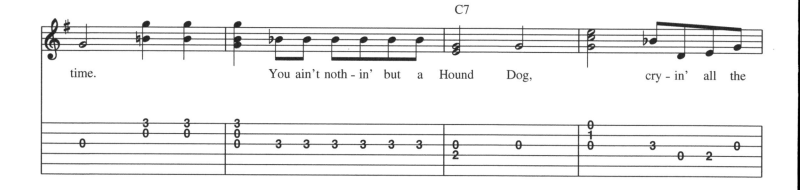

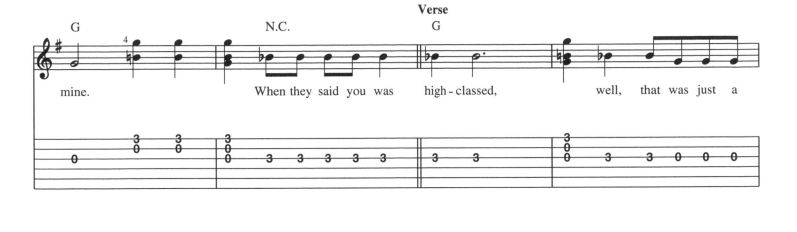

mine.

When they said you was high-classed, well, that was just a

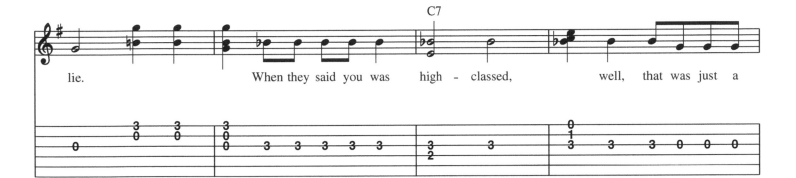

lie.

When they said you was high-classed, well, that was just a

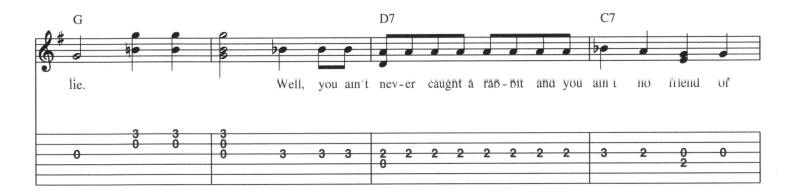

lie.

Well, you ain't nev-er caught a rab-bit and you ain't no friend of

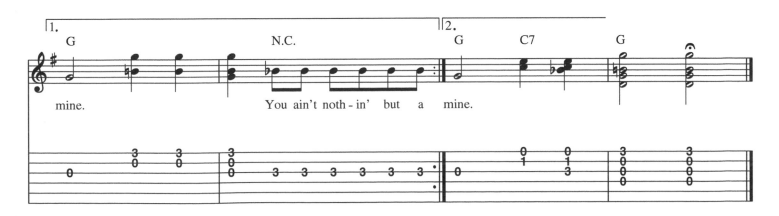

mine.

You ain't noth-in' but a mine.

Jailhouse Rock

Words and Music by Jerry Leiber and Mike Stoller

Strum Pattern: 3
Pick Pattern: 3

Chorus

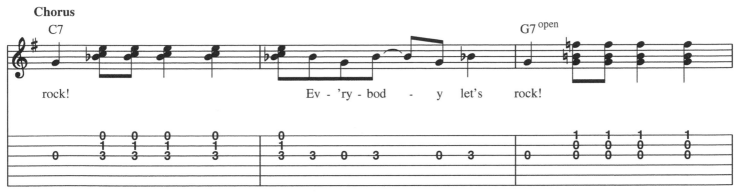

rock!   Ev - 'ry - bod - y let's   rock!

To Coda ⊕

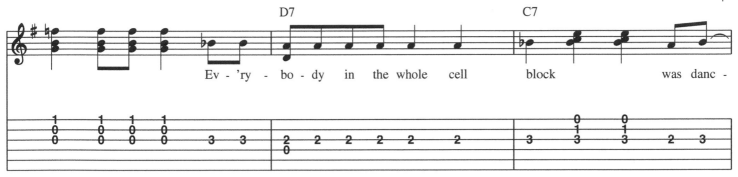

Ev - 'ry - bo - dy in the whole cell   block   was danc -

1., 2., 3.	4.		⊕ **Coda**	*Repeat and fade*
	D.S. al Coda		**Outro**	

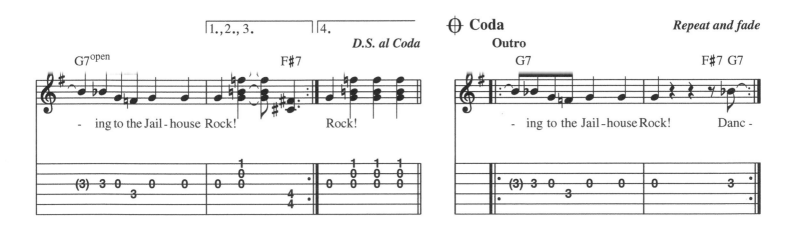

- ing to the Jail - house Rock!   Rock!   - ing to the Jail - house Rock!   Danc -

---

Additional Lyrics

2. Spider Murphy played the tenor saxophone,
   Little Joe was blowin' on the slide trombone.
   The drummer boy from Illinois went crash, boom, bang;
   The whole rhythm section was the Purple Gang.

3. Number Forty-seven said to number Three:
   "You're the cutest jailbird I ever did see.
   I sure would be delighted with your company,
   Come on and do the Jailhouse Rock with me."

4. The sad sack was a-sittin' on a block of stone,
   Way over in the corner weeping all alone.
   The warden said: "Hey, Buddy, don't you be no square,
   If you can't find a partner, use a wooden chair!"

5. Shifty Henry said to Bugs: "For heaven's sake,
   No one's lookin', now's our chance to make a break."
   Bugsy turned to Shifty and he said: "Nix, nix;
   I wanna stick around a while and get my kicks."

Kansas City

Words and Music by Jerry Leiber and Mike Stoller

Strum Pattern: 2, 3
Pick Pattern: 3, 4

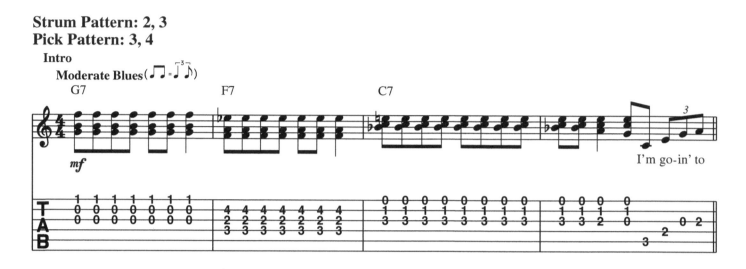

Verse

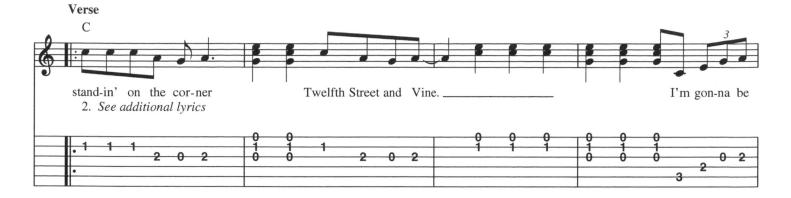

stand-in' on the cor-ner   Twelfth Street and Vine. _____   I'm gon-na be
2. *See additional lyrics*

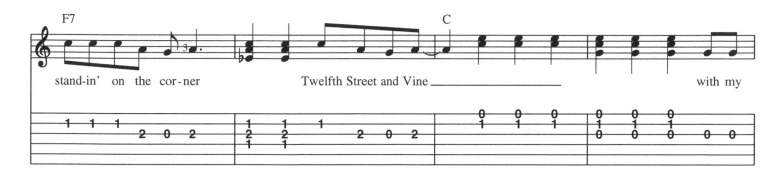

stand-in' on the cor-ner   Twelfth Street and Vine _____   with my

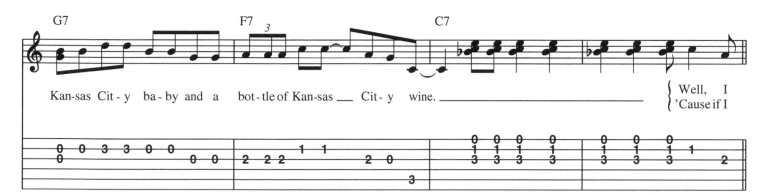

Kan-sas Cit-y ba-by and a bot-tle of Kan-sas ___ Cit-y wine. _____   { Well, I
                                                                                 { 'Cause if I

Bridge

might take a train, ___ I might take a plane, ___ but if I have to walk I'm
stay with that wom - an, I know I'm gon-na die. Got-ta find a brand new ba-by and

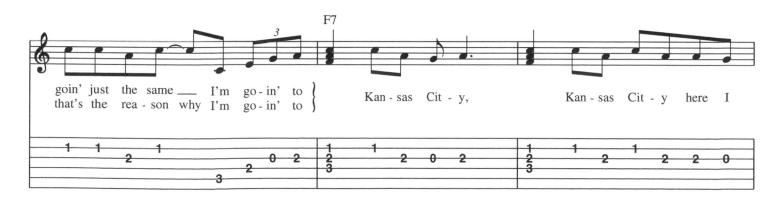

goin' just the same ___ I'm go-in' to }   Kan - sas Cit - y,   Kan - sas Cit - y here I
that's the rea - son why I'm go-in' to }

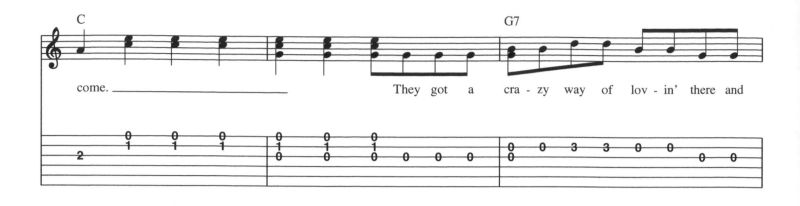

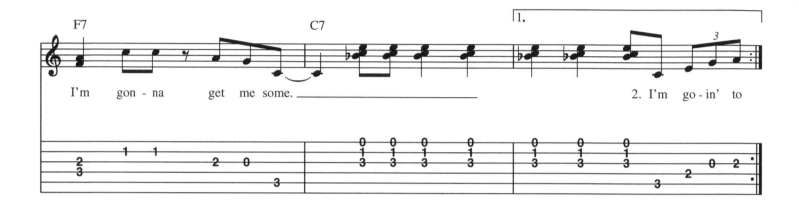

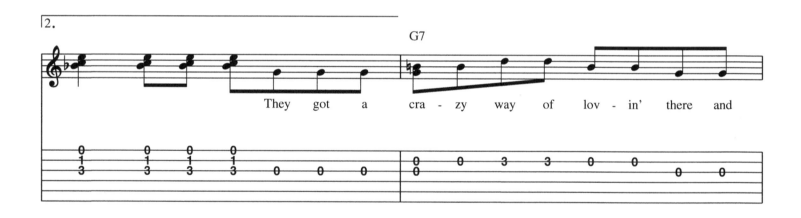

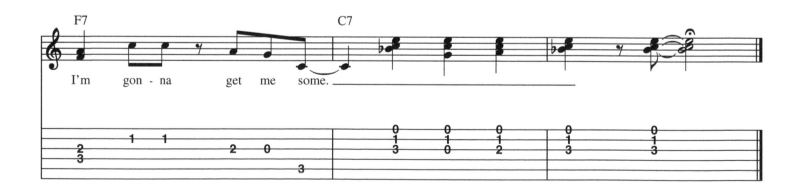

Additional Lyrics

2. I'm goin' to pack my clothes, leave at the crack of dawn.
   I'm goin' to pack my clothes, leave at the crack of dawn.
   My old lady will be sleepin' and she won't know where I've gone.

Matchbox

Words and Music by Carl Lee Perkins

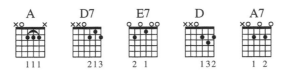

Strum Pattern: 1, 3
Pick Pattern: 1, 3

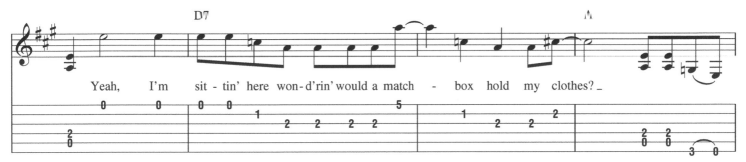

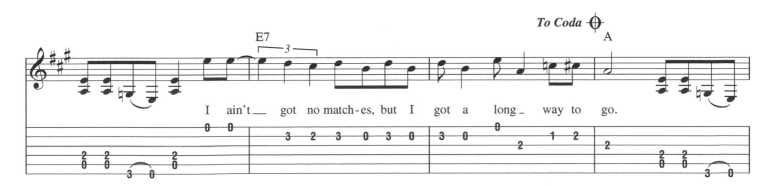

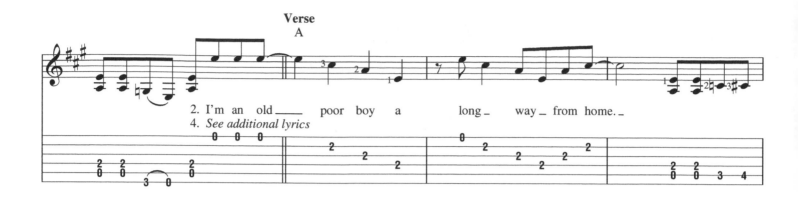

Verse

2. I'm an old___ poor boy a long___ way___ from home.___
4. *See additional lyrics*

I'm an old___ poor boy a long_____ way from home.

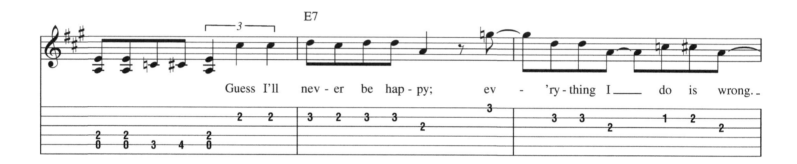

Guess I'll nev - er be hap - py; ev - 'ry-thing I___ do is wrong.___

Guitar Solo

Yeah!

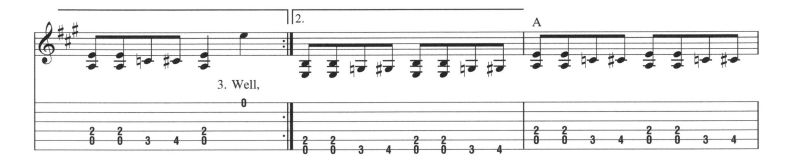

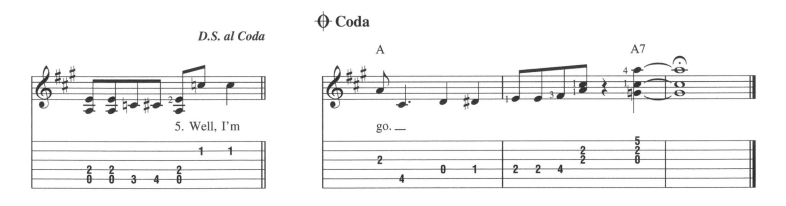

Additional Lyrics

3. Well, let me be your little dog, till your big dog come.
   Let me be your little dog, till your big dog come.
   When the big dog gets here, show him what this little puppy done.

4. Well, I'm sittin' here wond'rin' would a matchbox hold my clothes?
   Yeah. I'm sittin' here wond'rin' would a matchbox hold my clothes?
   I ain't got no matches, I got a long way to go.
   Spoken: Let her go, boy. Go, go!

La Bamba

By Ritchie Valens

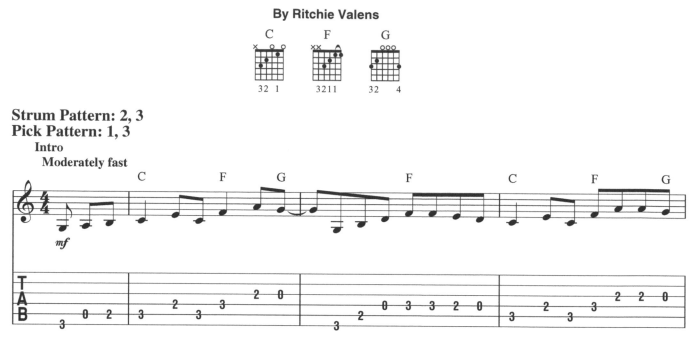

Strum Pattern: 2, 3
Pick Pattern: 1, 3

Intro
Moderately fast

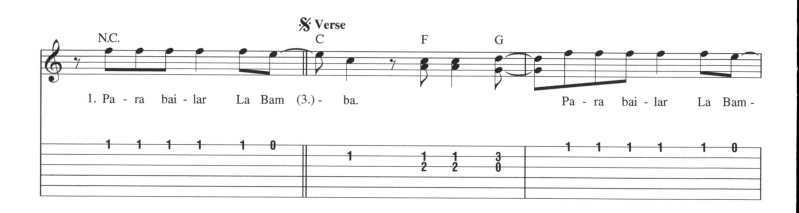

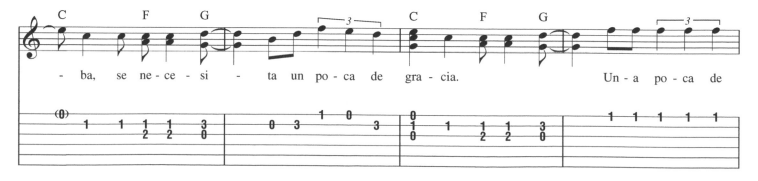

1. Pa - ra bai - lar La Bam (3.) - ba. Pa - ra bai - lar La Bam - ba, se ne - ce - si - ta un po - ca de gra - cia. Un - a po - ca de

To Coda ⊕

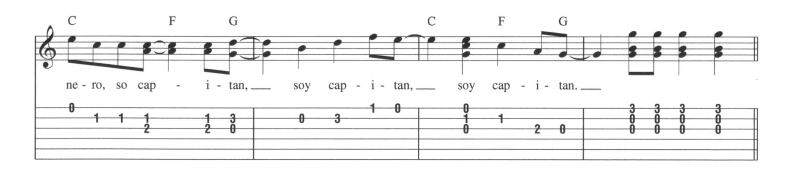

Chorus

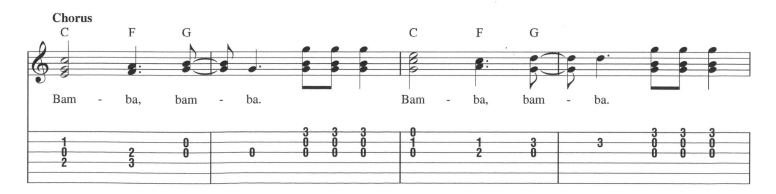

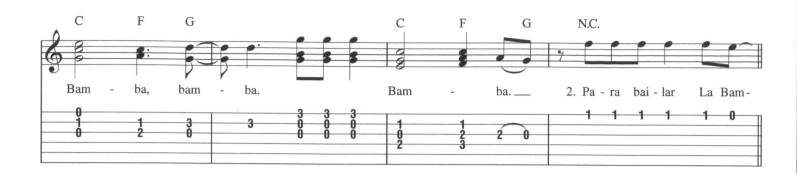

Bam - ba, bam - ba. Bam - ba. 2. Pa - ra bai - lar La Bam-

Verse

- ba. Pa - ra bai - lar La Bam - ba, se ne - ce - si-

- ta un po - ca de gra - cia. Un - a po - ca de

gra - cia pa - ra mi pa - ra ti y ar - ri - ba, ar - ri-

Guitar Solo

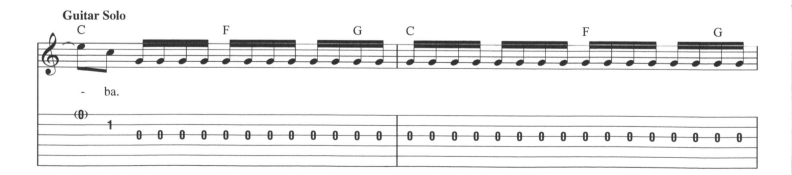

- ba.

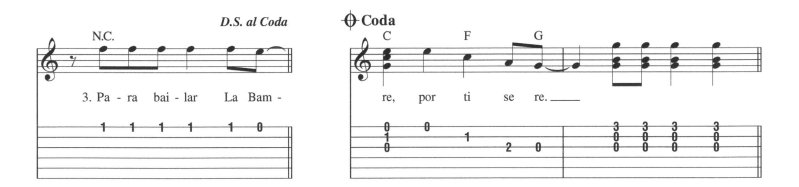

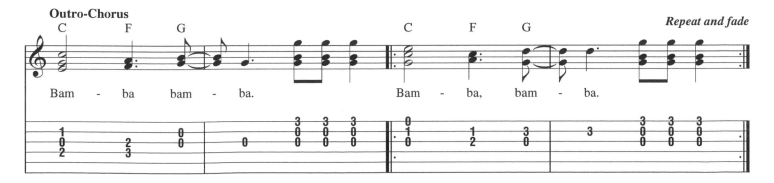

Long Tall Sally

Words and Music by Enotris Johnson, Richard Penniman and Robert Blackwell

3.

Outro

Yeah! _____ We're gon - na have some fun to - night, _____ gon - na

have some fun to - night, ___ woo! ___ We're gon - na have some fun to - night,_

_____ ev - 'ry - thing will be all right. _____ We're gon - na

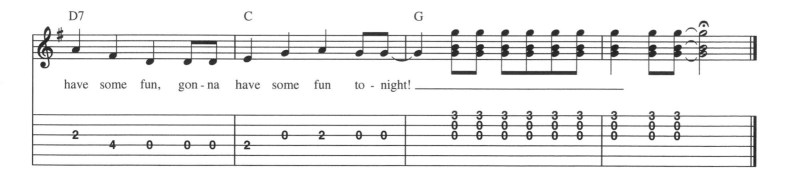

have some fun, gon - na have some fun to - night! _____

Additional Lyrics

2. Well, Long Tall Sally has a lot on the ball,
   And nobody cares if she's long and tall.

3. Well, I saw Uncle John with Long Tall Sally,
   He saw Aunt Mary comin' and he ducked back in the alley.

Mystery Train

Words and Music by Sam C. Phillips and Herman Parker Jr.

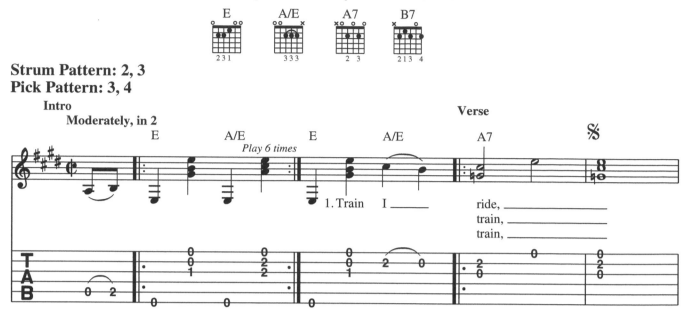

Strum Pattern: 2, 3
Pick Pattern: 3, 4

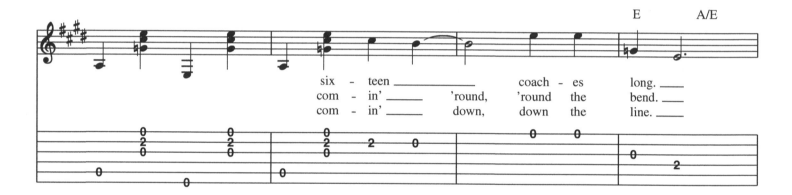

six - teen _____ coach - es long. ____
com - in' _____ 'round, 'round the bend. ____
com - in' _____ down, down the line. ____

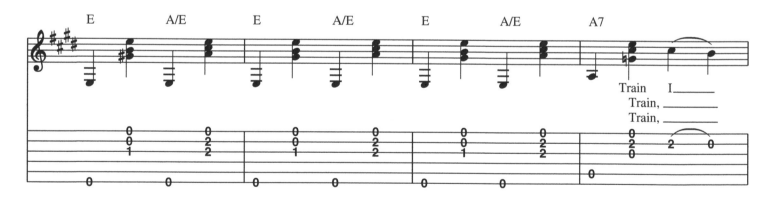

Train I _____
Train, _____
Train, _____

ride, _____   six - teen _____ coach - es
train, _____   com - in' _____ 'round _____ the
train, _____   com - in' _____ down _____ the

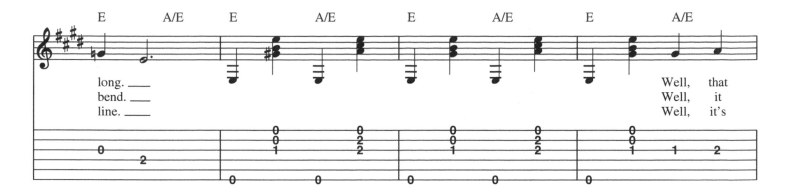

E   A/E   E   A/E   E   A/E   E   A/E

long. _____   Well,   that
bend. _____   Well,   it
line. _____   Well,   it's

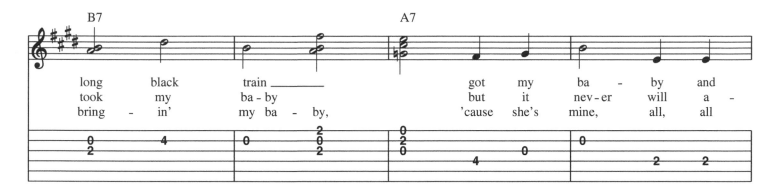

B7   A7

long   black   train _____   got   my   ba – by   and
took   my   ba – by,   but   it   nev – er   will   a –
bring – in'   my ba – by,   'cause   she's   mine,   all,   all

To Coda ⊕

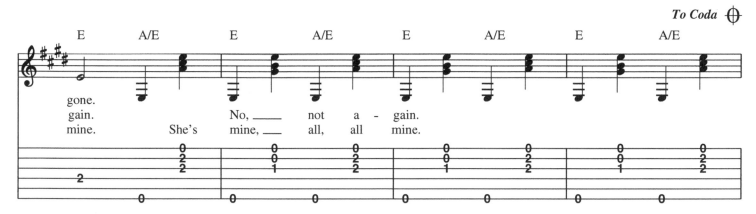

E   A/E   E   A/E   E   A/E   E   A/E

gone.
gain.   No, _____ not   a – gain.
mine.   She's   mine, ___ all,   all   mine.

D.S. al Coda
(2nd verse)

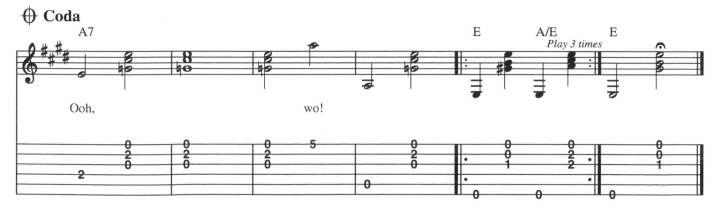

1., 2.   3.
A7   E   A/E   *Play 4 times*   E   A/E   A7

2. Train, _____   Train, _____   train, ___
3. Train, _____

⊕ **Coda**

A7   E   A/E   E
                                                    Play 3 times

Ooh,   wo!

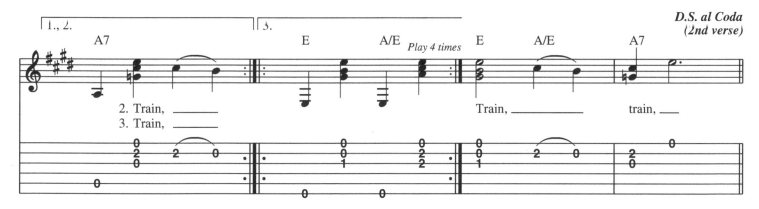

Peggy Sue

Words and Music by Jerry Allison, Norman Petty and Buddy Holly

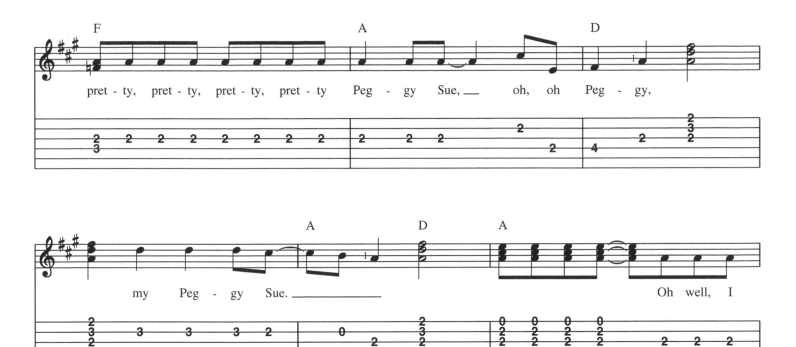

pret - ty, pret - ty, pret - ty, pret - ty Peg - gy Sue, ___ oh, oh Peg - gy,

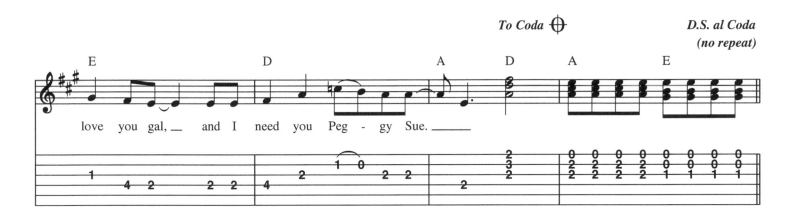

my Peg - gy Sue. _____ Oh well, I

To Coda ⊕

D.S. al Coda
(no repeat)

love you gal, __ and I need you Peg - gy Sue. ___

⊕ **Coda**

Oh well, I love you gal, __ and I want you Peg - gy Sue. __

Additional Lyrics

2. Peggy Sue, Peggy Sue,
   Oh how my heart yearns for you,
   Oh Peggy, my Pa-heggy Sue.
   Oh well, I love you gal, Peggy Sue.

3. I love you, Peggy Sue,
   With a love so rare and true,
   Oh Peggy, my Peggy Sue.
   Oh well, I love you gal, I want you Peggy Sue.

Ramrod

By Al Casey

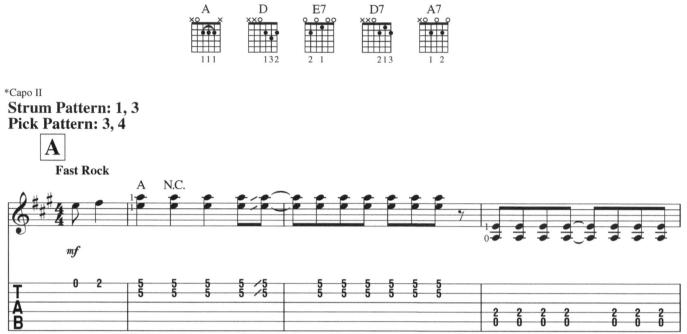

*Capo II

Strum Pattern: 1, 3
Pick Pattern: 3, 4

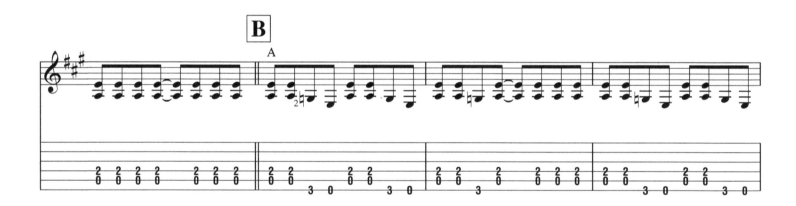

*Optional: To match recording, place capo at 2nd fret.

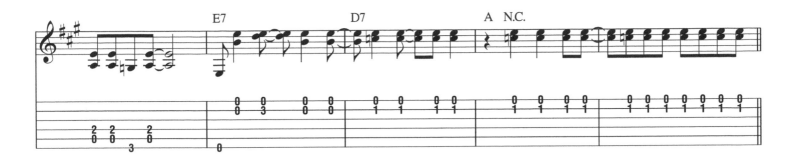

*Saxophone arranged for gtr.

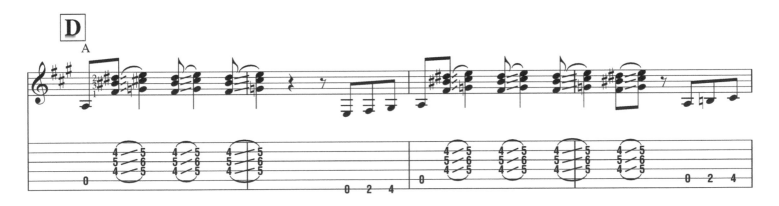

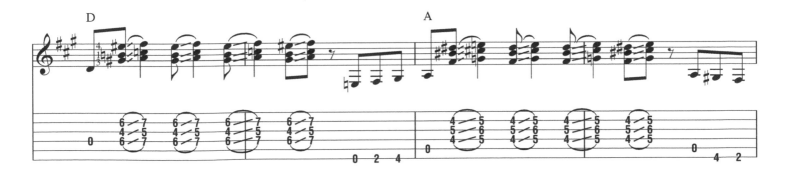

*Saxophone arranged for gtr.

E

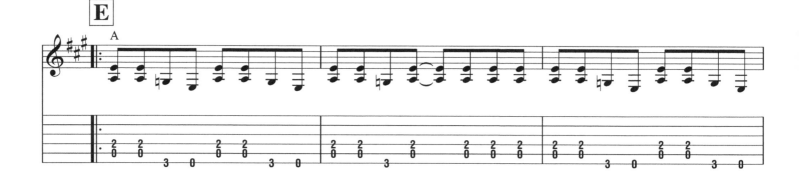

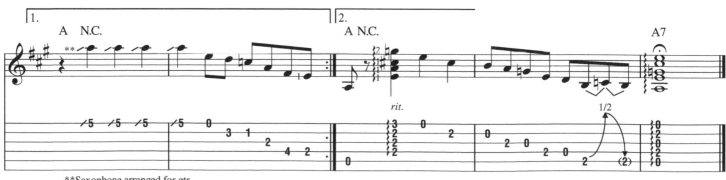

**Saxophone arranged for gtr.

Raunchy

By William Justis and Sidney Manker

Strum Pattern: 5
Pick Pattern: 1

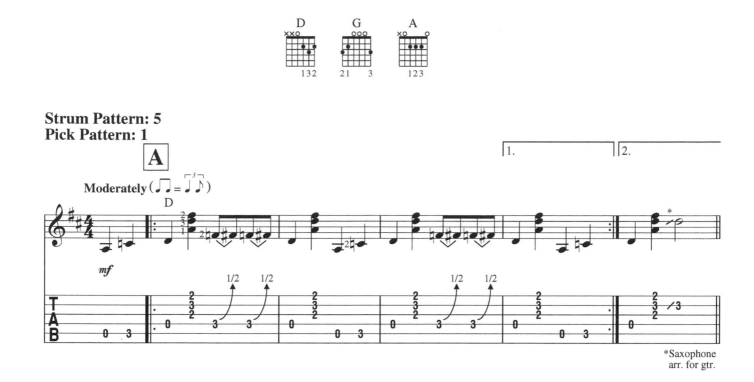

*Saxophone
arr. for gtr.

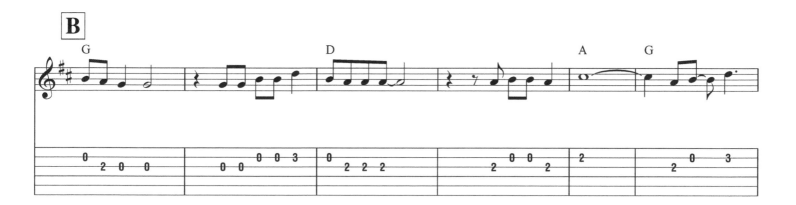

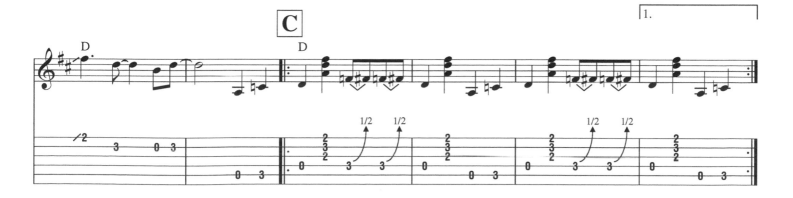

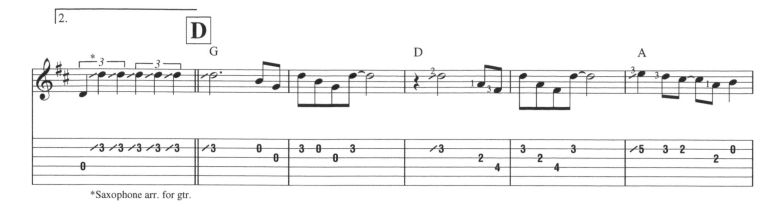

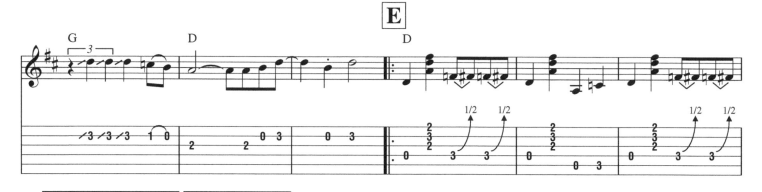

*Saxophone arr. for gtr.

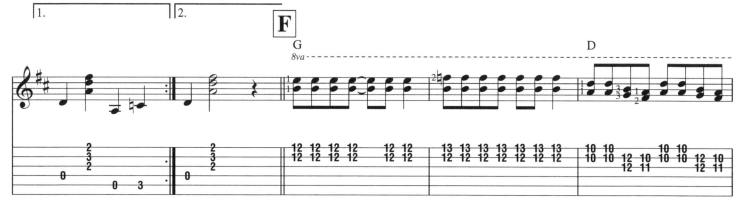

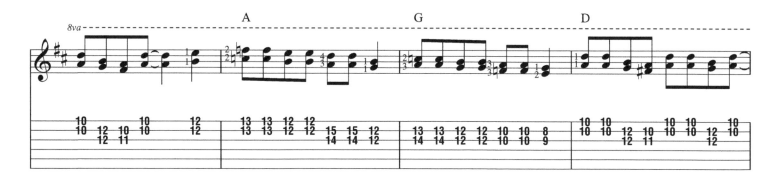

*Piano arr. for gtr.

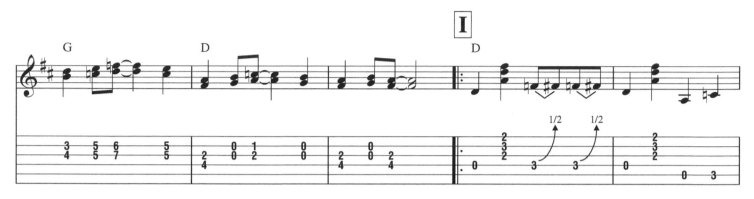

**Saxophone arr. for gtr.

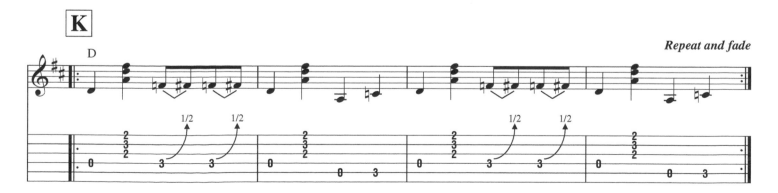

Rebel 'Rouser

By Duane Eddy and Lee Hazlewood

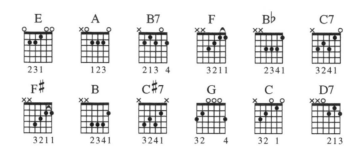

Strum Pattern: 4
Pick Pattern: 3

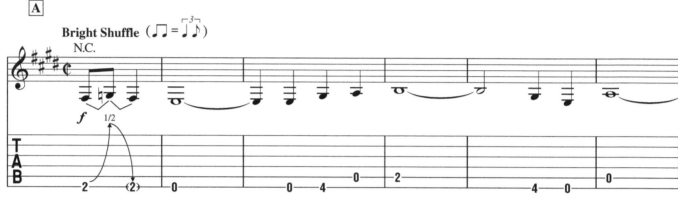

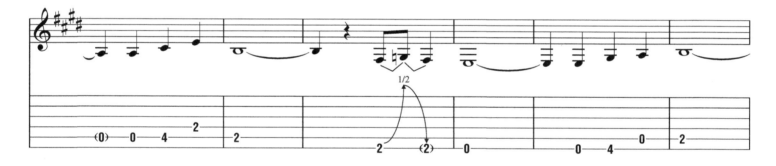

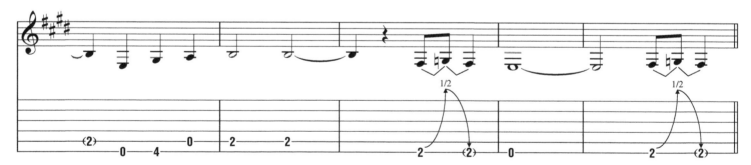

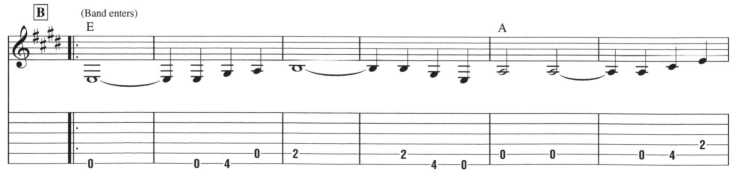

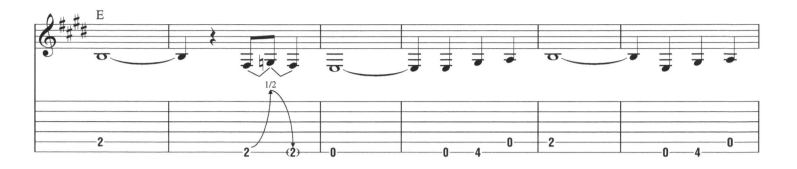

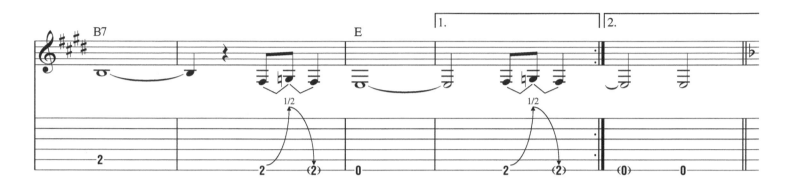

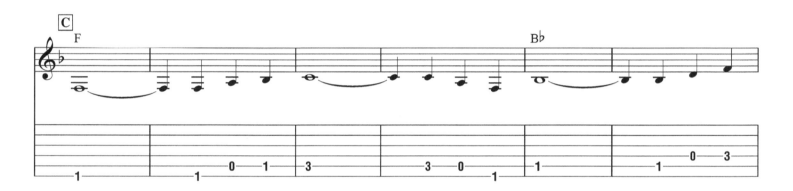

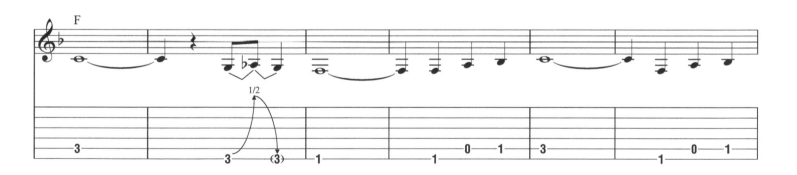

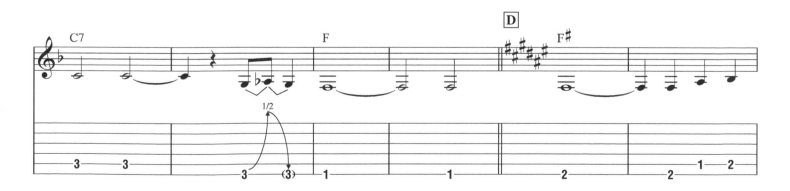

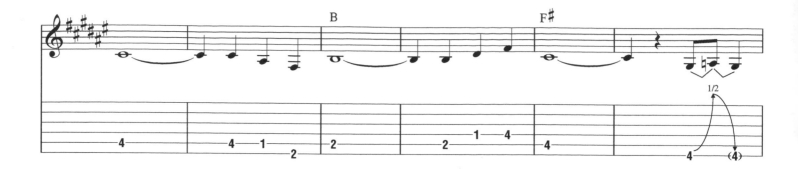

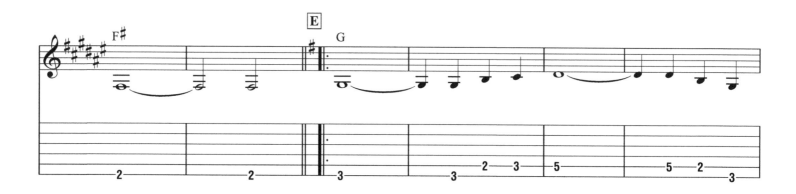

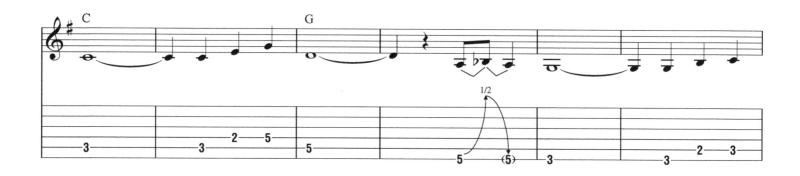

Rockin' Robin

Words and Music by J. Thomas

_____ to hear the rob - in go - in' tweet, tweet, tweet. Rock - in'

Chorus

rob - in, rock, rock, _____ rock - in' rob - in.

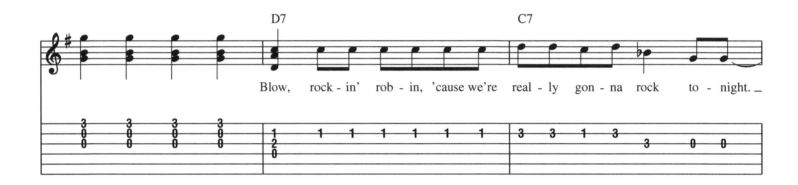

Blow, rock - in' rob - in, 'cause we're real - ly gon - na rock to - night. _____

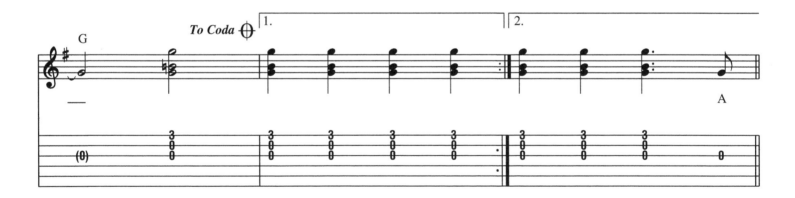

_____

Bridge

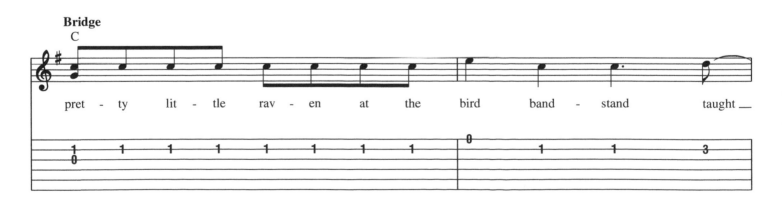

pret - ty lit - tle rav - en at the bird band - stand taught _____

him how to do the bop and it was grand. They

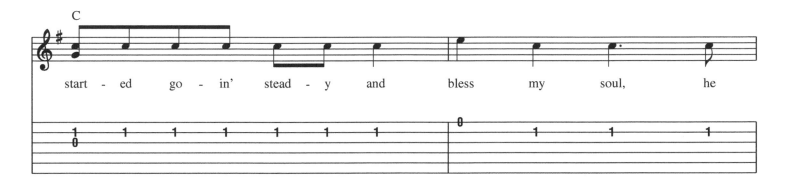

start - ed go - in' stead - y and bless my soul, he

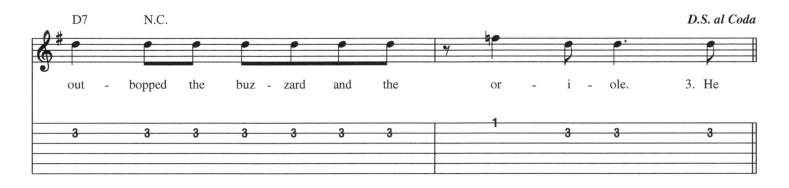

out - bopped the buz - zard and the or - i - ole. 3. He

D.S. al Coda

⊕ Coda

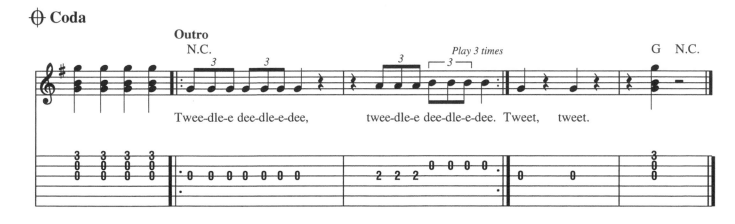

Outro

Play 3 times

Twee-dle-e dee-dle-e-dee, twee-dle-e dee-dle-e-dee. Tweet, tweet.

Additional Lyrics

2. Ev'ry little swallow, ev'ry chickadee,
   Ev'ry little bird in the tall oak tree.
   The wise old owl, the big black crow,
   Flap their wings singin' go, bird, go.

Red River Rock

Written by Tom King, Ira Mack and Fred Mendelsohn

*Capo II

Strum Pattern: 2
Pick Pattern: 4

Moderately bright Rock

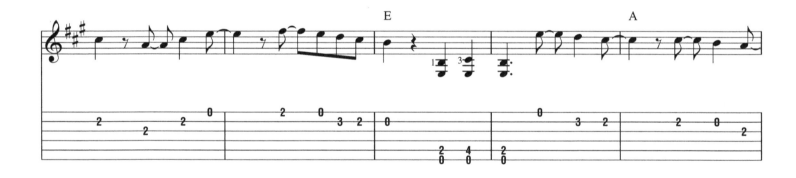

*Optional: To match recording, place capo at 2nd fret.

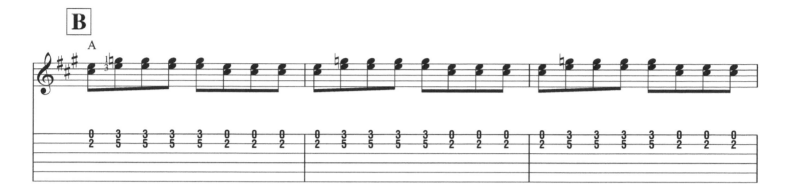

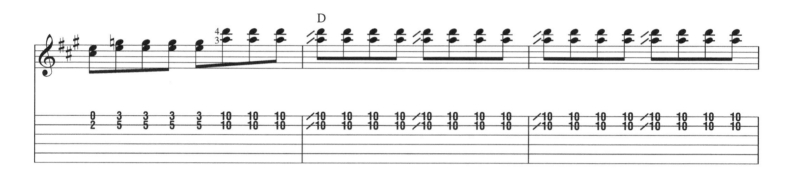

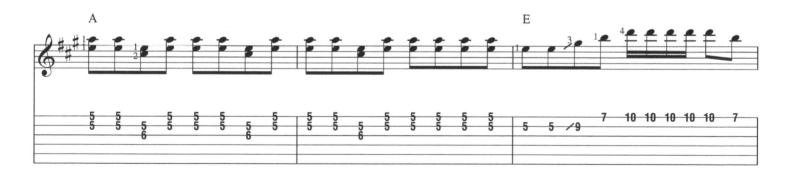

D.S. and fade
(take repeat)

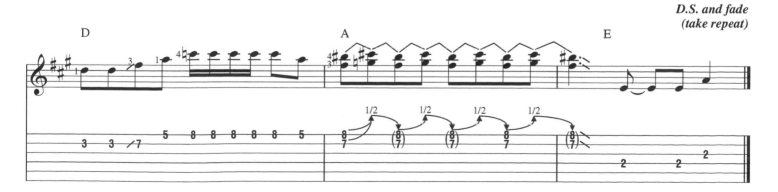

Rock and Roll Is Here to Stay

Words and Music by David White

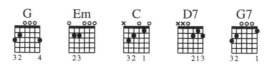

Strum Pattern: 3
Pick Pattern: 3

Intro

Moderately, in 2

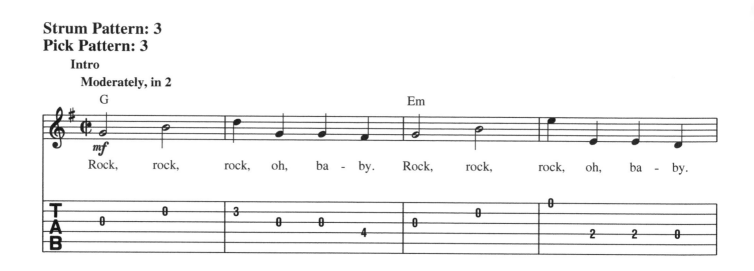

Rock, rock, rock, oh, ba - by. Rock, rock, rock, oh, ba - by.

Rock, rock, rock, oh, ba - by. Rock, rock, rock, oh, ba - by...

To Coda

Verse

1. Rock and roll is here to stay, and it will nev - er die. _____
3. *See additional lyrics*

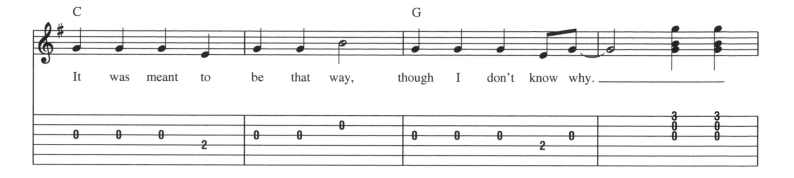

It was meant to be that way, though I don't know why. _____

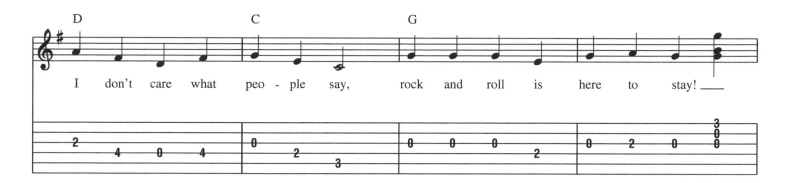

I don't care what peo - ple say, rock and roll is here to stay! ____

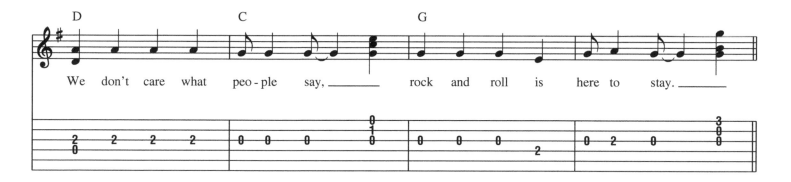

We don't care what peo - ple say, _____ rock and roll is here to stay. _____

Verse

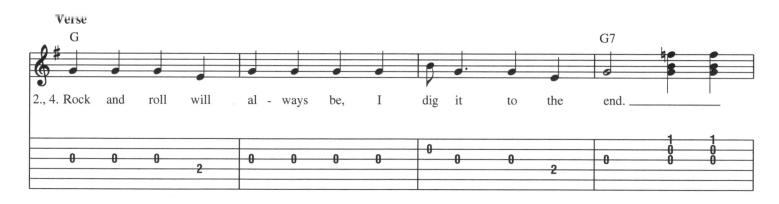

2., 4. Rock and roll will al - ways be, I dig it to the end. _____

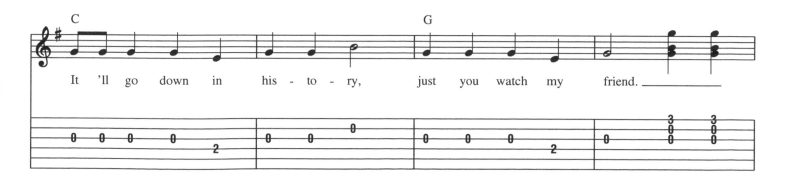

It 'll go down in his - to - ry, just you watch my friend. _____

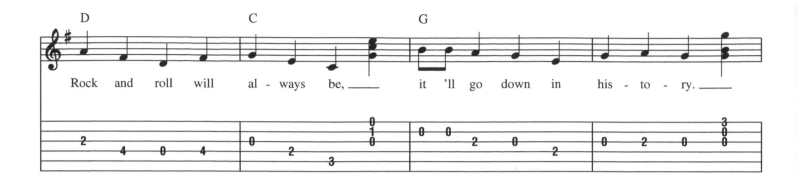

Chorus

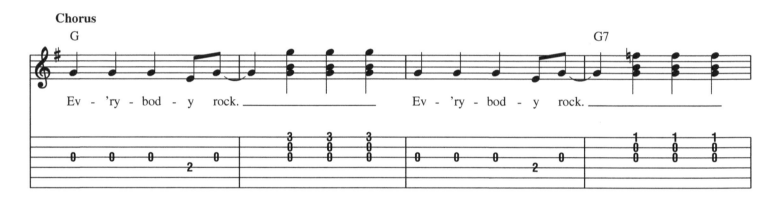

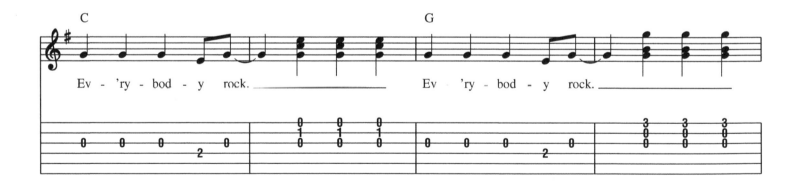

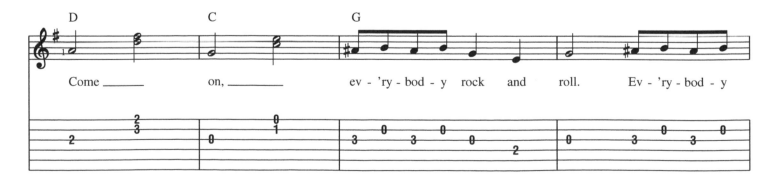

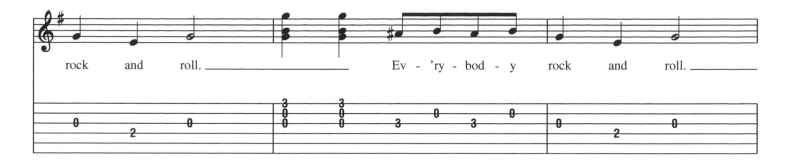

rock and roll. _____ Ev - 'ry - bod - y rock and roll. _____

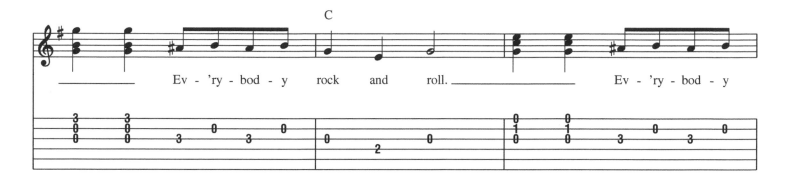

_____ Ev - 'ry - bod - y rock and roll. _____ Ev - 'ry - bod - y

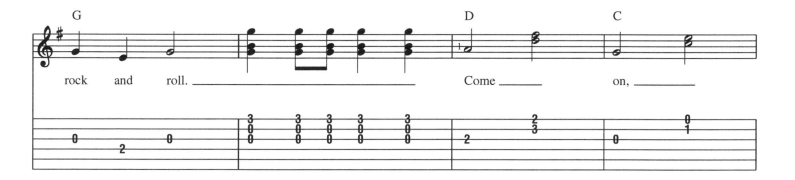

rock and roll. _____ Come _____ on, _____

⊕ **Coda**

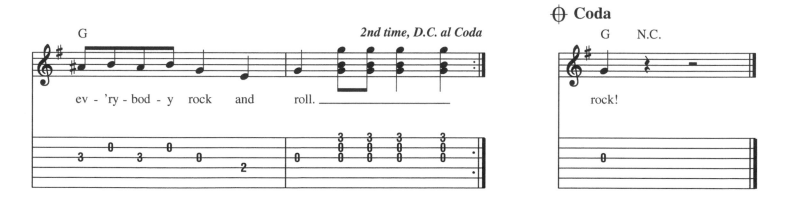

2nd time, D.C. al Coda

ev - 'ry - bod - y rock and roll. _____

rock!

Additional Lyrics

3. If you don't like rock and roll, just think what you've been missin'.
   But if you like to bop and stroll, walk around and listen.
   Let's all start to rock and roll, ev'rybody rock and roll.

Rock Around the Clock

Words and Music by Max C. Freedman and Jimmy DeKnight

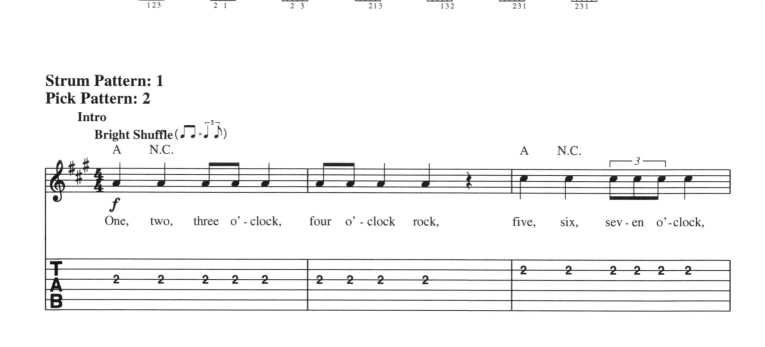

Strum Pattern: 1
Pick Pattern: 2

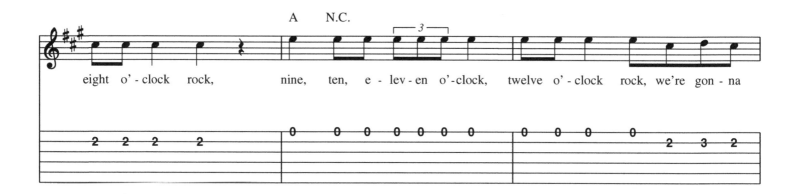

One, two, three o'-clock, four o'-clock rock, five, six, sev-en o'-clock,

eight o'-clock rock, nine, ten, e-lev-en o'-clock, twelve o'-clock rock, we're gon-na

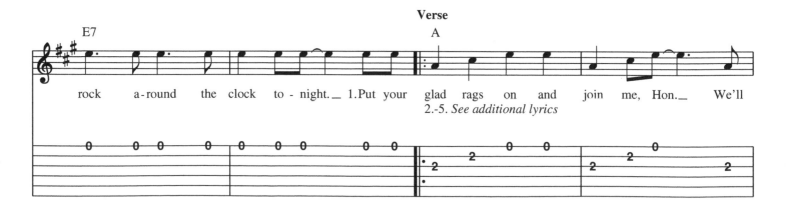

rock a-round the clock to-night.__ 1.Put your glad rags on and join me, Hon.__ We'll
2.-5. *See additional lyrics*

have some fun when the clock strikes one. __ We're gon - na rock a - round the

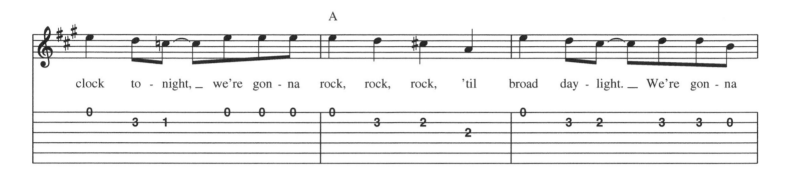

clock to - night, __ we're gon - na rock, rock, rock, 'til broad day - light. __ We're gon - na

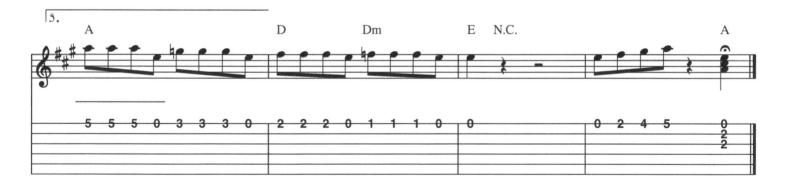

rock, gon - na rock a - round __ the clock __ to - night. _____ 2. When the

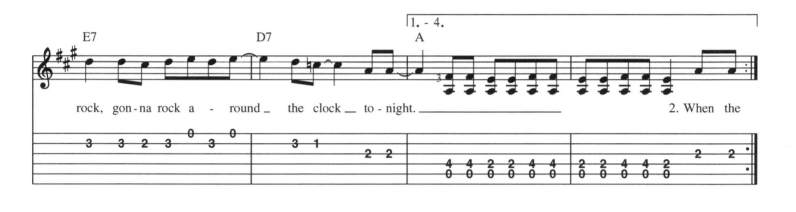

Additional Lyrics

2. When the clock strikes two, and three and four,
   If the band slows down we'll yell for more.
   We're gonna rock around the clock tonight,
   We're gonna rock, rock, rock, 'til broad daylight.
   We're gonna rock, gonna rock around the clock tonight.

3. When the chimes ring five and six and seven,
   We'll be rockin' up in seventh heav'n.
   We're gonna rock around the clock tonight,
   We're gonna rock, rock, rock, 'til broad daylight.
   We're gonna rock, gonna rock around the clock tonight.

4. When it's eight, nine, ten, eleven, too,
   I'll be goin' strong and so will you.
   We're gonna rock around the clock tonight,
   We're gonna rock, rock, rock, 'til broad daylight.
   We're gonna rock, gonna rock around the clock tonight.

5. When the clock strikes twelve, we'll cool off, then,
   Start a rockin' 'round the clock again.
   We're gonna rock around the clock tonight,
   We're gonna rock, rock, rock, 'til broad daylight.
   We're gonna rock, gonna rock around the clock tonight.

Rocket 88

Words and Music by Jackie Brenston

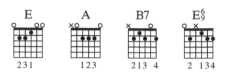

*Tune down 1/2 step:
(low to high) E♭-A♭-D♭-G♭-B♭-E♭

Strum Pattern: 1, 3
Pick Pattern: 3, 5

*Optional: To match recording, tune down 1/2 step.

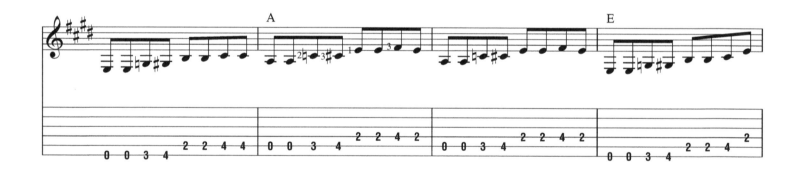

§ § **Verse**

1. You wom-en have heard of jal - op - ies, you've heard the noise they make. But let me _
3. *See additional lyrics*

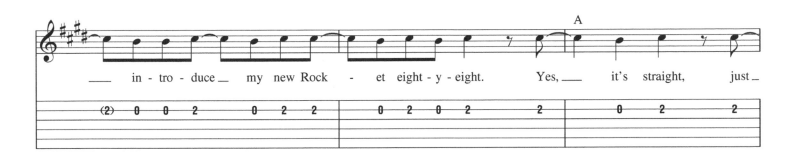

___ in - tro - duce ___ my new Rock - et eight - y - eight. Yes, ___ it's straight, just ___

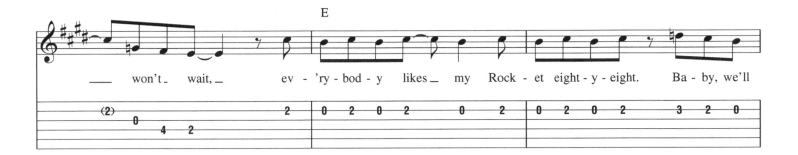

___ won't _ wait, _ ev - 'ry - bod - y likes _ my Rock - et eight - y - eight. Ba - by, we'll

To Coda 2 ⊕

ride in style, _ mov - in' all ___ a - long. ___

⊕ **Coda 1**

D.S. al Coda 1

Verse

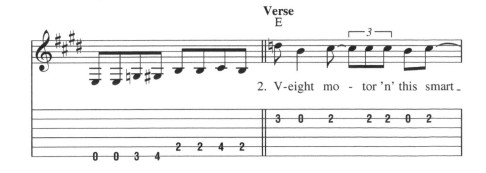

2. V-eight mo - tor 'n' this smart _

___ 'n' de - sign, black con - vert - i - ble top ___ an' the gals ___ don't ___ mind. _

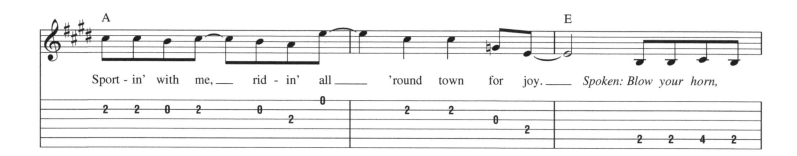

Sport - in' with me, ___ rid - in' all ___ 'round town for joy. ___ *Spoken: Blow your horn,*

Saxophone Solo

Ray - mond, blow it!

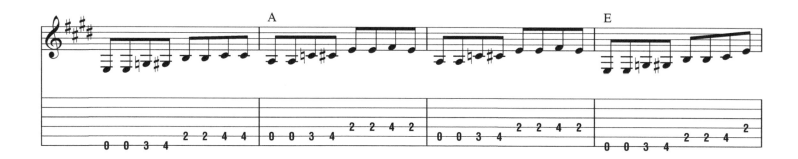

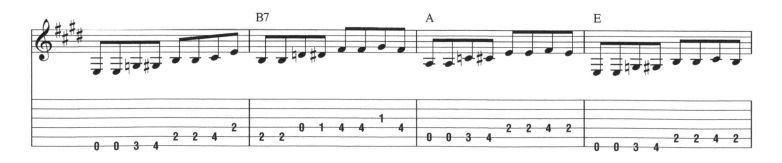

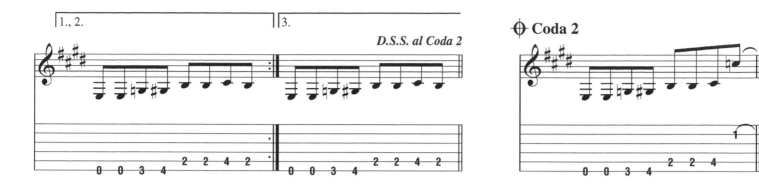

Additional Lyrics

3. Step in my Rocket and don't be late,
   Baby, we're pullin' out about half past eight.
   Goin' 'round the corner and get a fifth.
   Ev'rybody, my car's gonna take a little nip.
   Move on out, boozin' 'n' cruisin' along.

See You Later, Alligator

Words and Music by Robert Guidry

*Tune down 1/2 step:
(low to high) E♭-A♭-D♭-G♭-B♭-E♭

Strum Pattern: 1, 3
Pick Pattern: 1, 3

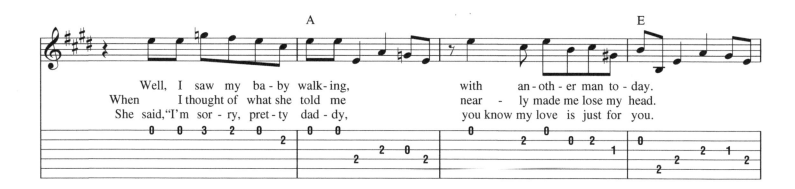

*Optional: To match recording, tune down 1/2 step.

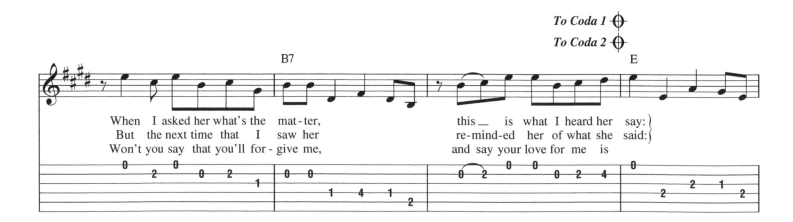

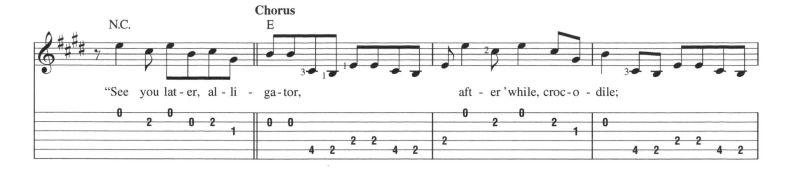

"See you lat - er, al - li - ga - tor, aft - er 'while, croc - o - dile;

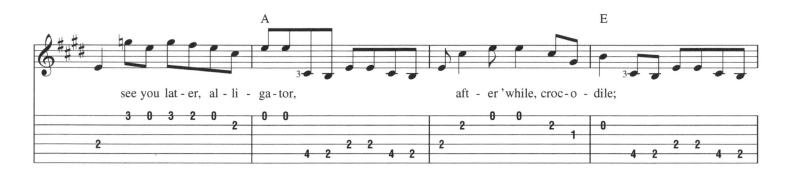

see you lat - er, al - li - ga - tor, aft - er 'while, croc - o - dile;

Can't you see you're in my way, now? Don't you know you cramp my style?"

2. When I thought of what she style? 3. *Instrumental*

Instrumental ends

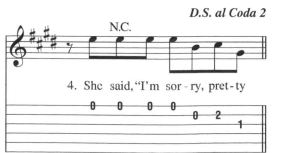

4. She said, "I'm sor - ry, pret - ty

true?" 5. I said, "A wait a min - ute,

Verse

'ga - tor, I know you mean it just for play.

I said, "Wait a min - ute, 'ga - tor, I know you mean it just for

play. Don't you know you real - ly hurt me,

and this is what I have to say: See you lat - er, al - li -

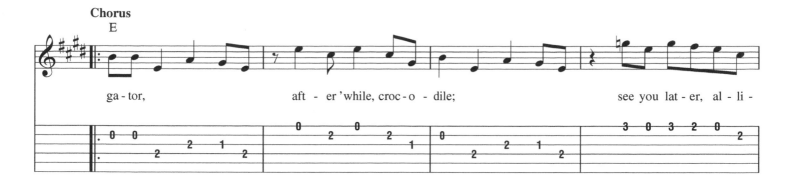

Chorus

ga - tor, aft - er 'while, croc - o - dile; see you lat - er, al - li -

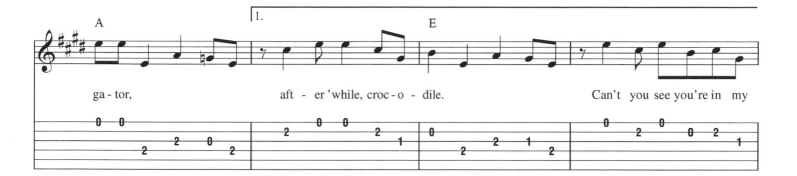

ga - tor, aft - er 'while, croc - o - dile. Can't you see you're in my

way, now? Don't you know you cramp my style?" See you lat - er, al - li -

so long, ___ that's all, ___ good - bye! ___

Shake, Rattle and Roll

Words and Music by Charles Calhoun

Strum Pattern: 3
Pick Pattern: 3

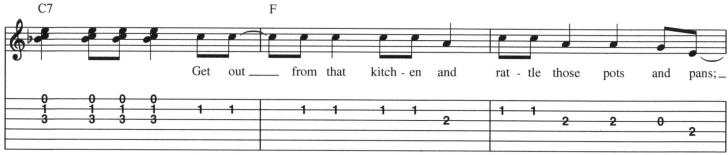

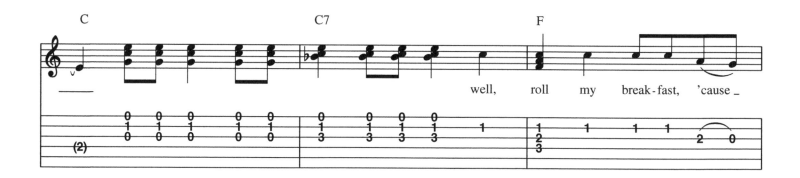

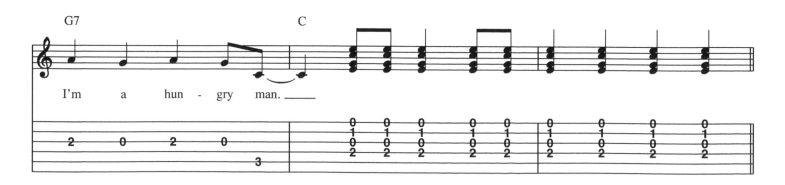

Chorus

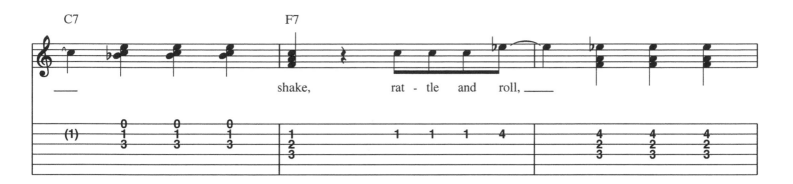

Shake,   rat - tle and roll, _____   shake,   rat - tle and roll, _

_   shake,   rat - tle and roll, _____

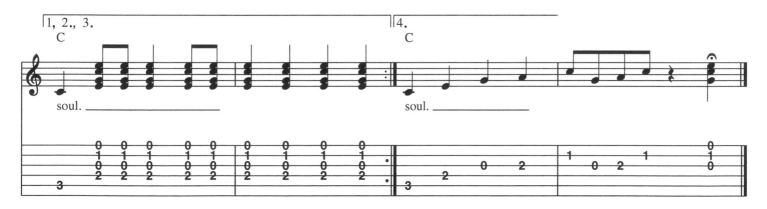

shake,   rat - tle and roll, _   you   nev - er do noth - in' to   save   your   dog - gone

|1, 2., 3. ||4.

soul. _____   soul. _____

Additional Lyrics

2. Wearin' those dresses, your hair done up so right.
   Wearin' those dresses, your hair done up so right;
   You look so warm, but your heart is cold as ice.

3. I'm like a one-eyed cat, peepin' in a seafood store.
   I'm like a one-eyed cat, peepin' in a seafood store;
   I can look at you, tell you don't love me no more.

4. I believe you're doing me wrong and now I know.
   I believe you're doing me wrong and now I know;
   The more I work, the faster my money goes.

Singing the Blues

Words and Music by Melvin Endsley

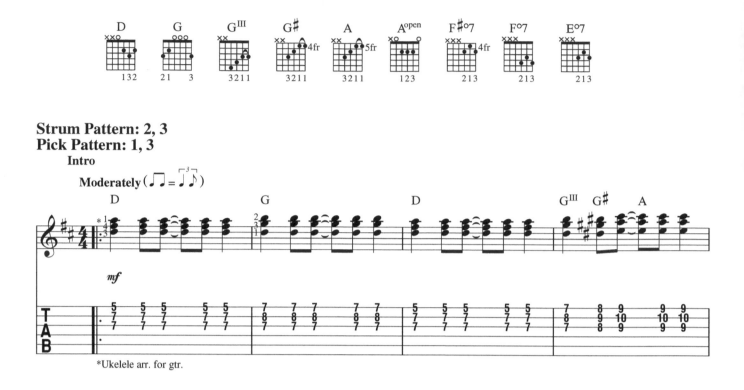

Strum Pattern: 2, 3
Pick Pattern: 1, 3

Intro

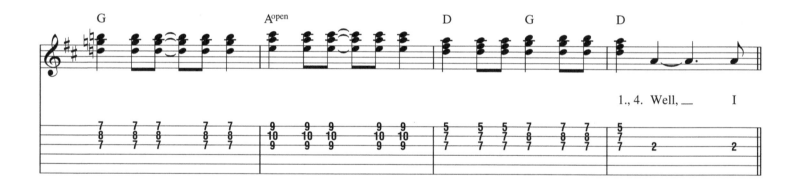

*Ukelele arr. for gtr.

Verse

nev-er felt more like sing — ing the blues, __ 'cause I nev-er thought __ that I'd ev-er lose __ your __

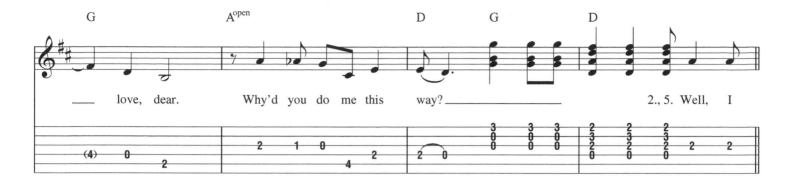

_____ love, dear. Why'd you do me this way? _____ 2., 5. Well, I

Verse

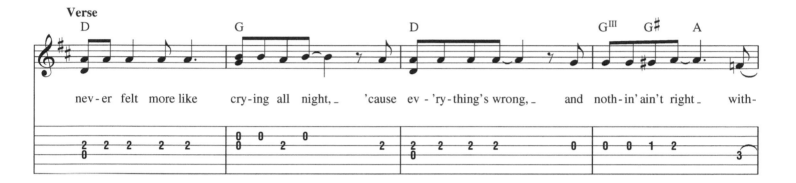

nev-er felt more like cry-ing all night, _ 'cause ev-'ry-thing's wrong, _ and noth-in' ain't right _ with-

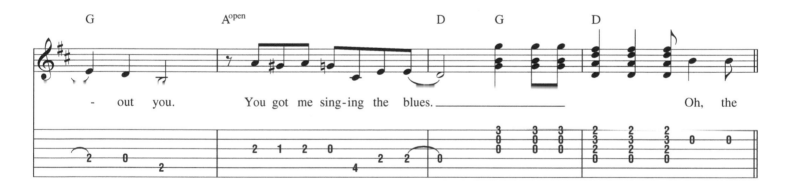

-out you. You got me sing-ing the blues. _____ Oh, the

Bridge

moon and stars _ no long-er shine. _ The dream is gone _ I thought was mine. _ There's

nothing left for me to do ___ but cry _____ o - ver you. ___

*Use Pattern 10

Verse

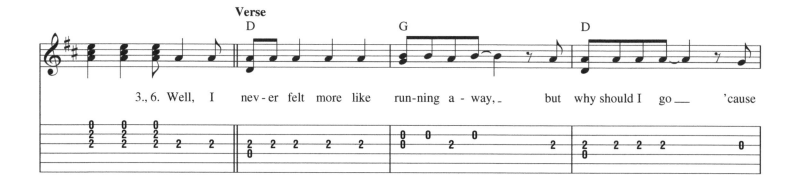

3., 6. Well, I nev-er felt more like run-ning a-way, ___ but why should I go ___ 'cause

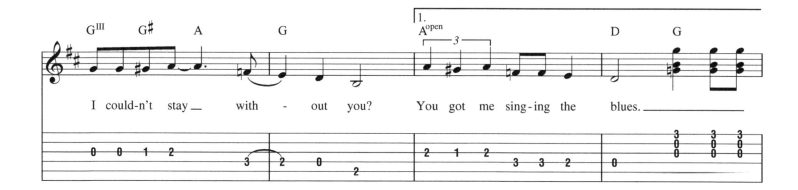

I could-n't stay ___ with - out you? You got me sing-ing the blues. _____

You got me sing-ing the blues. _____

Tequila

By Chuck Rio

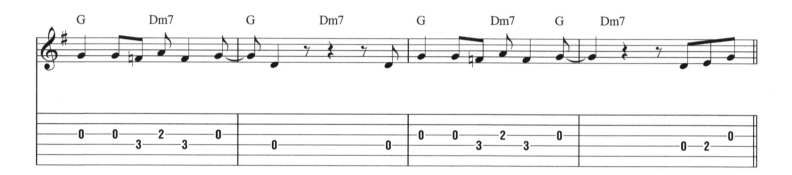

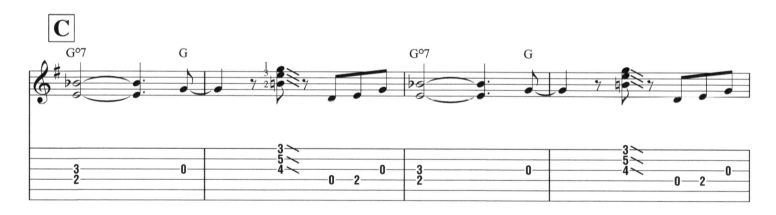

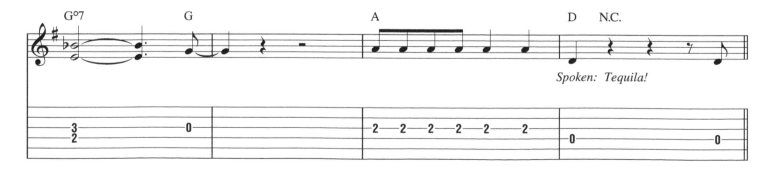

Spoken: Tequila!

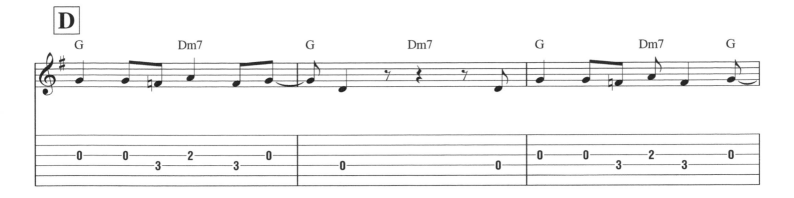

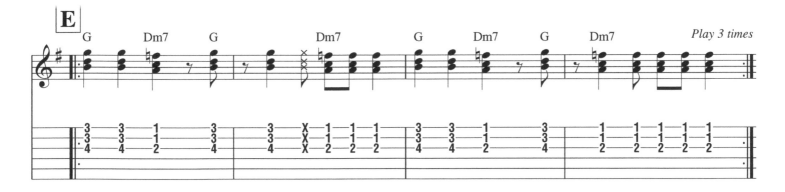

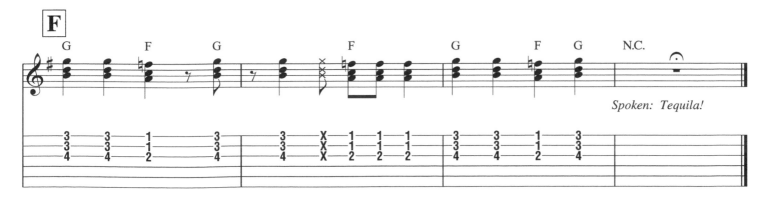

Sleepwalk

By Santo Farina, John Farina and Ann Farina

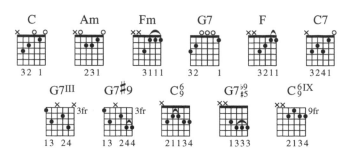

Strum Pattern: 8
Pick Pattern: 8

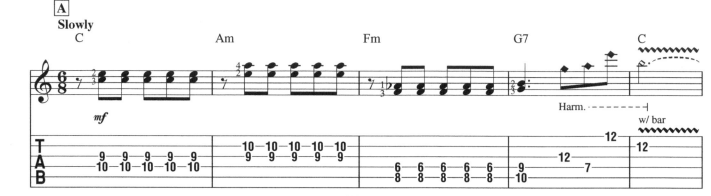

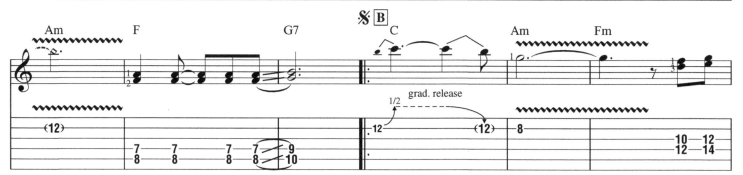

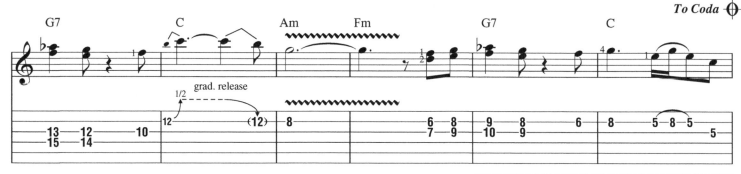

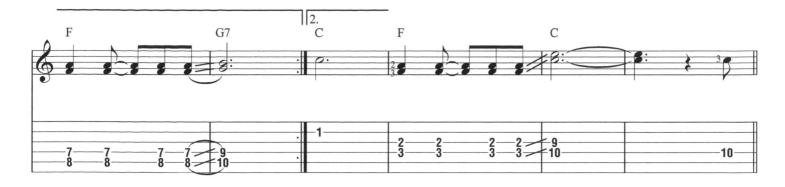

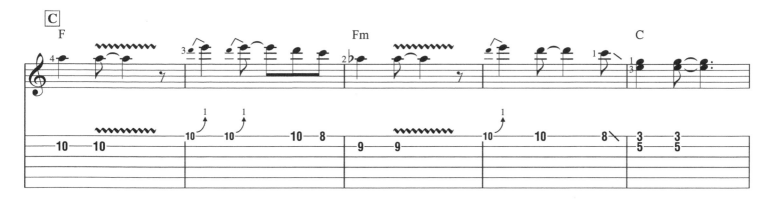

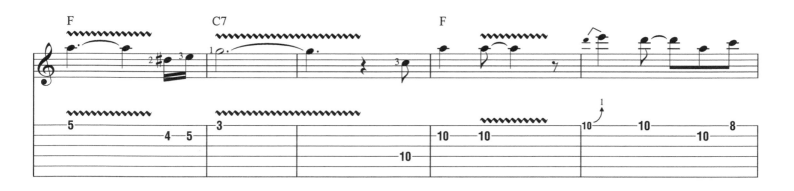

Splish Splash

Words and Music by Bobby Darin and Murray Kaufman

Strum Pattern: 1
Pick Pattern: 2

1. Splish splash, I was tak-in' a bath 'long a-bout a Sat-ur-day night.
2. *See additional lyrics*

A rub dub, just re-lax-in' in the tub, think-in' ev-'ry-thing was all right.

Well, I stepped out the tub put my feet on the floor, I wrapped the towel a-round me and I o-pened the door. And then a-splish splash, I

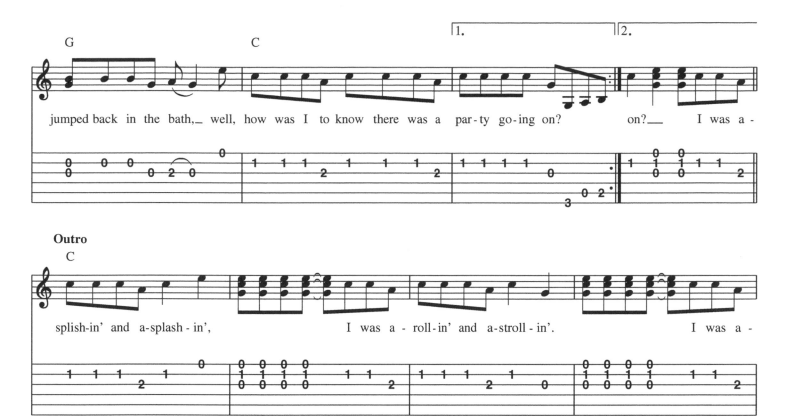

jumped back in the bath,_ well, how was I to know there was a par-ty go-ing on? on?_ I was a-

Outro

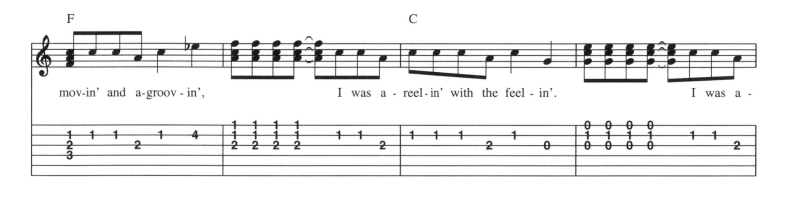

splish-in' and a-splash-in', I was a-roll-in' and a-stroll-in'. I was a-

mov-in' and a-groov-in', I was a-reel-in' with the feel-in'. I was a-

mov-in' and a groov-in', reel-in' with the feel-in'. Yeah, _____ splish, splash._

Additional Lyrics

2. Bing bang, I saw the whole gang,
Dancin' on my livin' room rug. Yeah.
Flip flop, they were doin' the bop,
All the teens had the dancin' bug.
There was Lollipop with Peggy Sue.
Good golly, Miss Molly was a-even there too.
A well a-splish splash, I forgot about the bath,
I went and put my dancing shoes on.

The Stroll

Words and Music by Clyde Otis and Nancy Lee

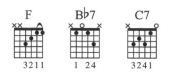

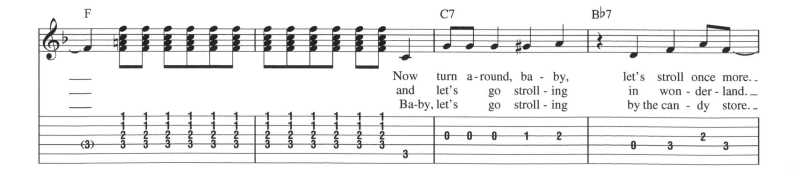

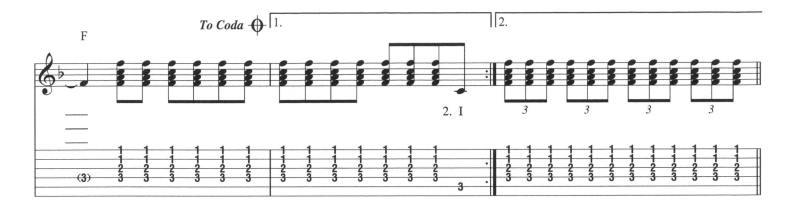

Chorus

Stroll - ing, __ whoa, yeah, __ stroll - ing, __ oh, oh, rock and roll -

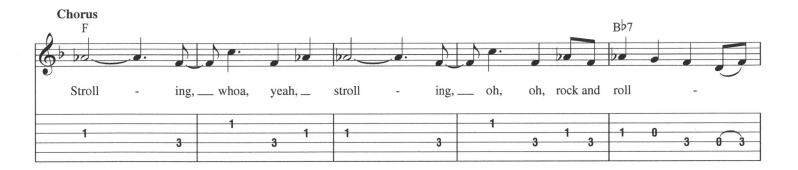

ing, stroll - ing. __ Well, a rock a my soul __

D.S. al Coda

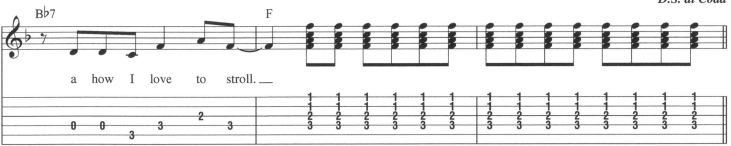

a how I love to stroll. __

Coda

Outro

Repeat and fade

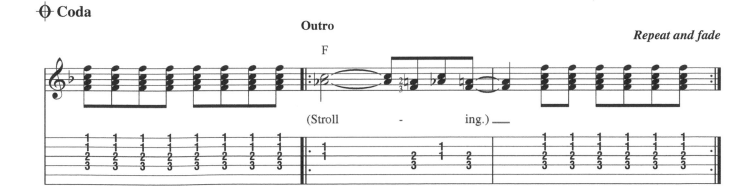

(Stroll - ing.) __

Summertime, Summertime

Words and Music by Tom Jameson and Sherm Feller

*Sung one octave higher throughout Verse.

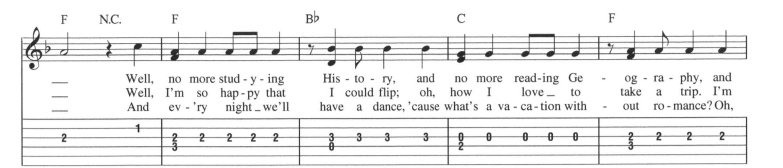

Well,   no more stud - y - ing   His - to - ry,   and   no more read-ing Ge   -   og - ra - phy, and
Well,   I'm so hap-py that   I could flip;   oh, how I   love _   to   take   a   trip. I'm
And   ev -'ry   night _ we'll   have   a   dance, 'cause what's a va - ca - tion with - out ro - mance? Oh,

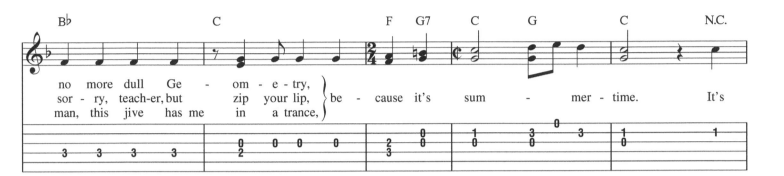

no more dull   Ge - om - e - try,
sor - ry,   teach-er, but   zip   your lip,   } be - cause   it's   sum - mer - time.   It's
man, this jive   has me   in   a trance,

time   to head straight   for   them hills.   It's   time   to live   and   have   some thrills.   Come a - long and

have   a   ball,   a   reg - u - lar ____   free - for - all.   { 2. Well,
                                                                    3. Well,   It's

Coda

sum-mer-time. _____   It's

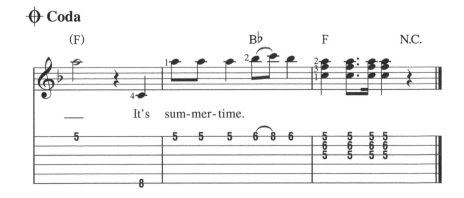

____   It's sum-mer-time.

Susie-Q

Words and Music by Dale Hawkins, Stan Lewis and Eleanor Broadwater

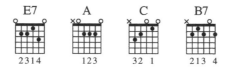

Strum Pattern: 4
Pick Pattern: 1, 4

1., 5. Oh, __ Su - sie - Q. __ Oh, __ Su - sie - Q.
3. *See additional lyrics*

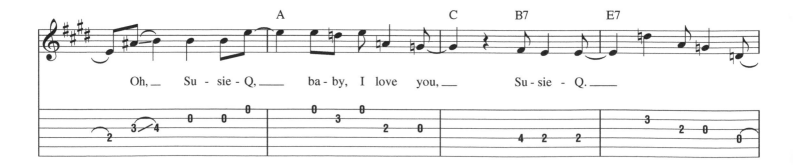

Oh, __ Su - sie - Q, __ ba - by, I love you, __ Su - sie - Q. __

Verse

2. Like the way you walk.___ I like the way you talk.___
4. *See additional lyrics*

To Coda 2 ⊕

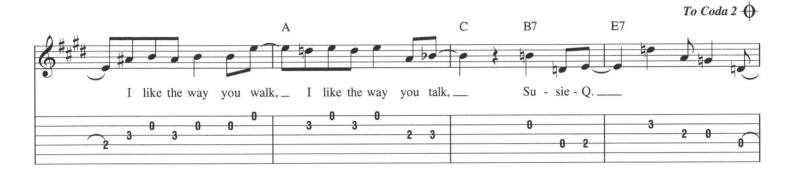

I like the way you walk,___ I like the way you talk,___ Su - sie - Q.___

To Coda 1 ⊕
Guitar Solo

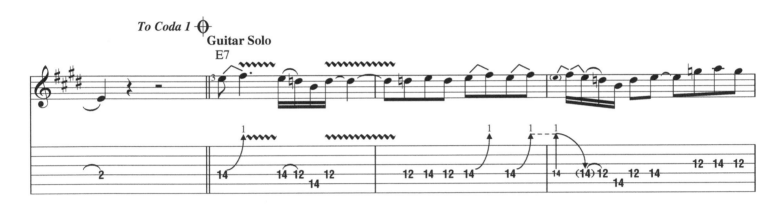

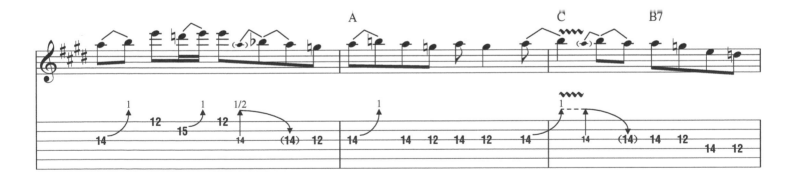

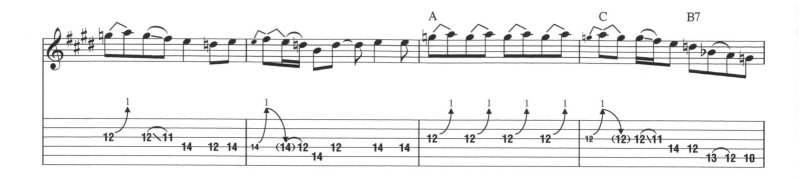

⊕ Coda 1

D.C. al Coda 1
(take repeat)

Guitar Solo

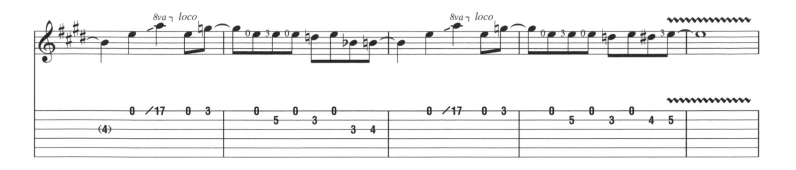

D.C. al Coda 2
(take repeat)

⊕ Coda 2

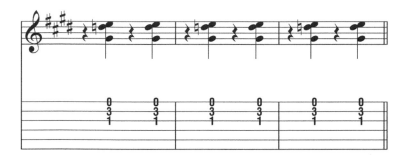

Verse

6. Oh, Su-sie - Q. ___

Oh, Su-sie - Q. ___   Oh, Su-sie - Q, ___ ba-by, I love you, ___ Su-sie - Q. ___

Outro

Repeat and fade

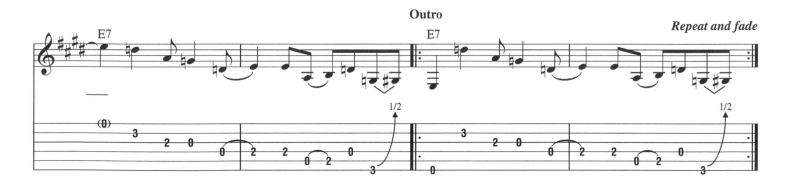

Additional Lyrics

3. Well, say that you'll be true.
   Well, say that you'll be true.
   Well, say that you'll be true
   And never leave me blue, Susie-Q.

4. Well, say that you'll be mine.
   Well, say that you'll be mine.
   Well, say that you'll be mine,
   Baby, all the time, Susie-Q.

A Teenager in Love

Words and Music by Doc Pomus and Mort Shuman

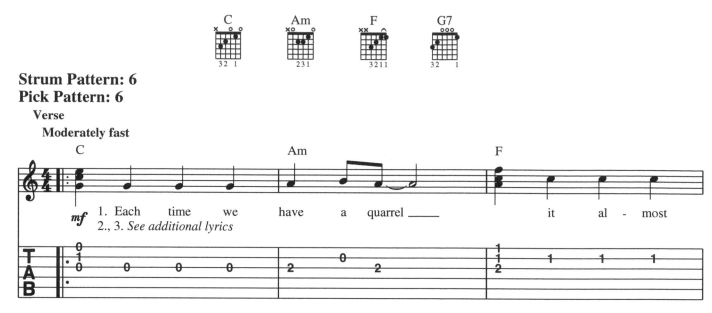

Strum Pattern: 6
Pick Pattern: 6

Verse

Moderately fast

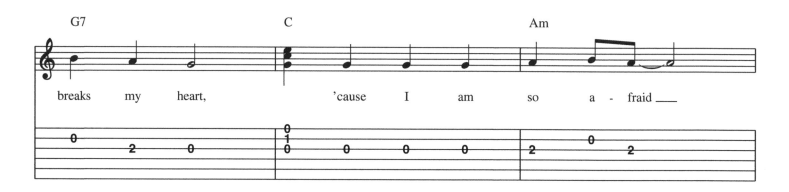

mf 1. Each time we have a quarrel ____ it al - most
2., 3. *See additional lyrics*

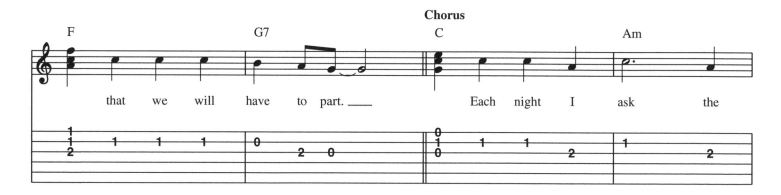

breaks my heart, 'cause I am so a - fraid ____

Chorus

that we will have to part. ____ Each night I ask the

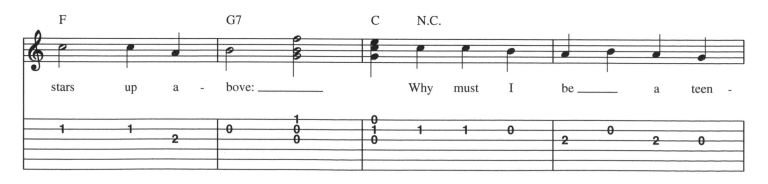

stars up a - bove: ____ Why must I be ____ a teen -

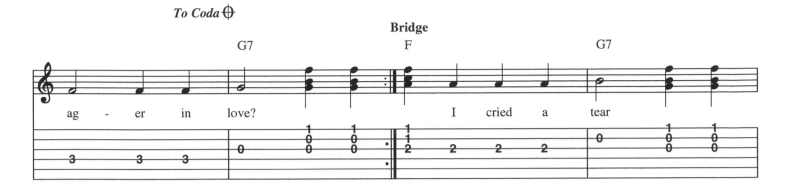

To Coda ⊕

Bridge

ag - er in love?   I cried a tear

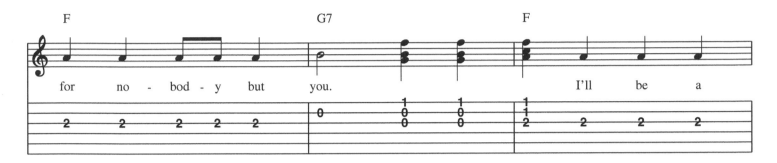

for no - bod - y but you.   I'll be a

D.C. al Coda

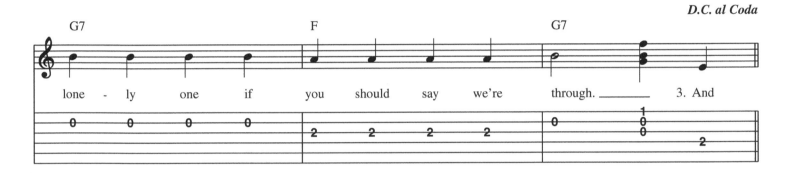

lone - ly one if you should say we're through. _____ 3. And

⊕ **Coda**

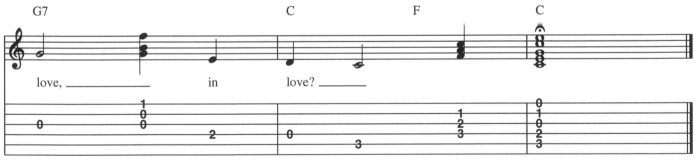

love, _____ in love? _____

Additional Lyrics

2. One day I feel so happy,
   Next day I feel so sad.
   I guess I'll learn to take
   The good with the bad.

3. And if you want to make me cry,
   That won't be so hard to do.
   And if you should say goodbye,
   I'll still go on loving you.

That'll Be the Day

Words and Music by Jerry Allison, Norman Petty and Buddy Holly

Strum Pattern: 1
Pick Pattern: 2

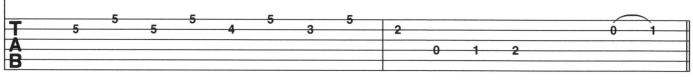

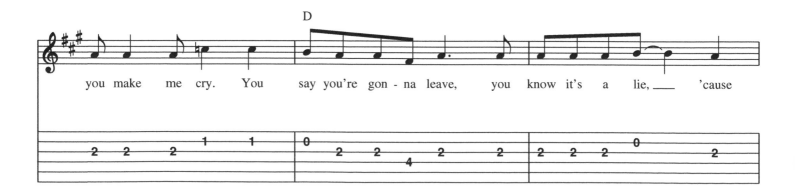

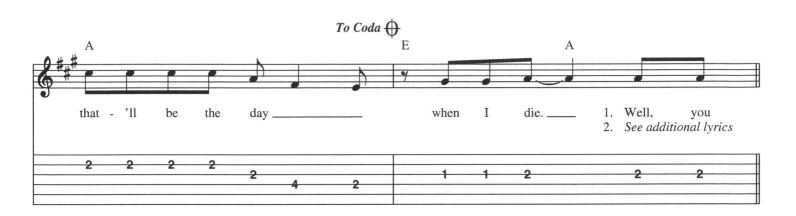

that -'ll be the day _____ when I die. ___ 1. Well, you
2. *See additional lyrics*

Verse

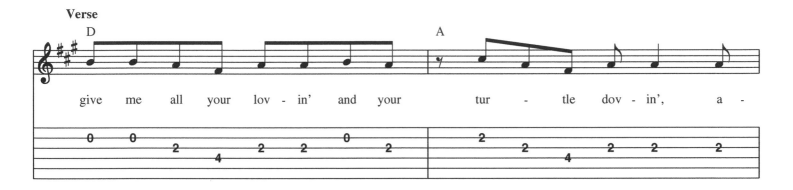

give me all your lov - in' and your tur - tle dov - in', a -

all your hugs and kiss - es and your mon - ey too. ___ Well, ___ a -

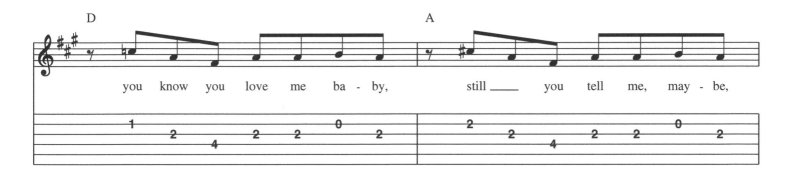

you know you love me ba - by, still ___ you tell me, may - be,

2nd time, D.S. al Coda

that some day, well, I'll be blue. Well, _____

⊕ Coda

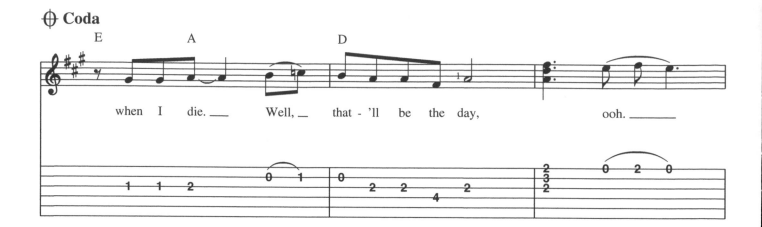

when I die. ___ Well, ___ that-'ll be the day, ooh. _____

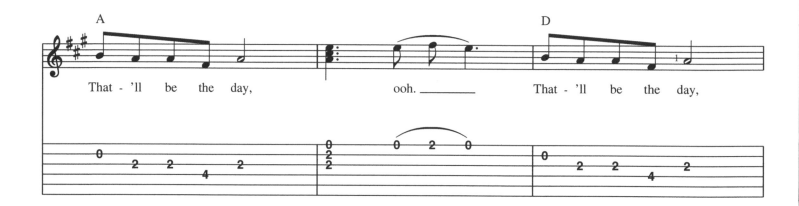

That-'ll be the day, ooh. _____ That-'ll be the day,

ooh. _____ That-'ll be the day.

Additional Lyrics

2. Well, when cupid shot his dart,
   He shot it at your heart,
   So if we ever part then I'll leave you.
   You sit and hold me and you
   Tell me boldly, that some day,
   Well, I'll be through.

Wake Up Little Susie

Words and Music by Boudleaux Bryant and Felice Bryant

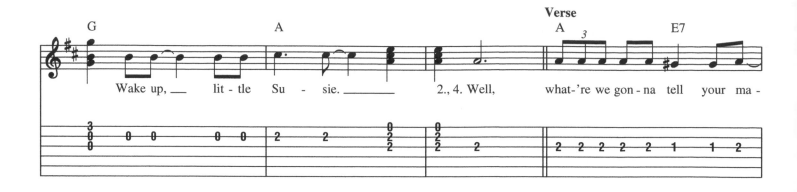

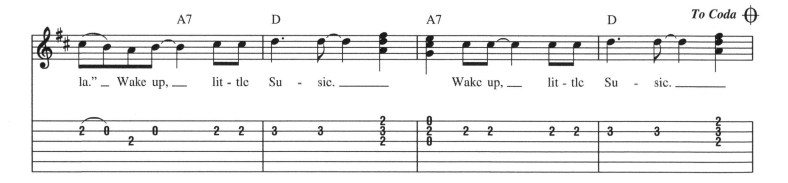

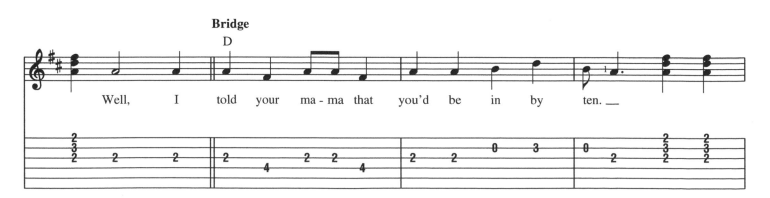

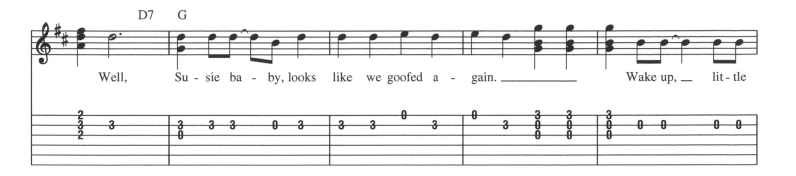

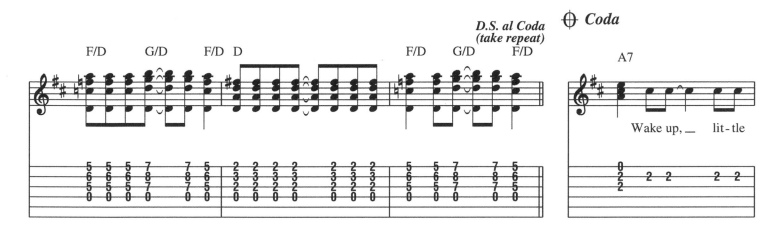

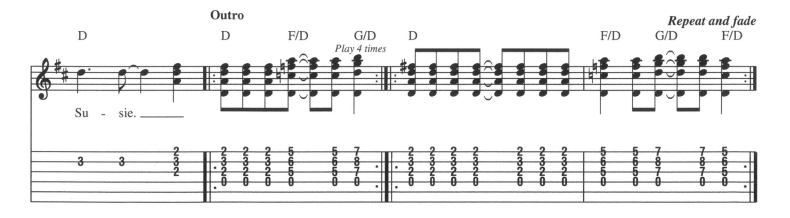

Additional Lyrics

3. The movie wasn't so hot.
It didn't have much of a plot.
We fell asleep, our goose is cooked,
Our reputation is shot.
Wake up, little Susie.
Wake up, little Susie.

That's All Right

Words and Music by Arthur Crudup

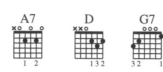

Strum Pattern: 3, 4
Pick Pattern: 3, 5

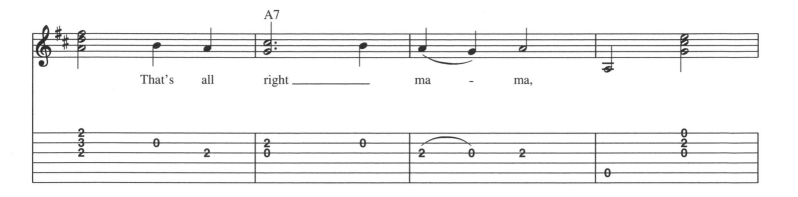

That's all right _____ ma - ma,

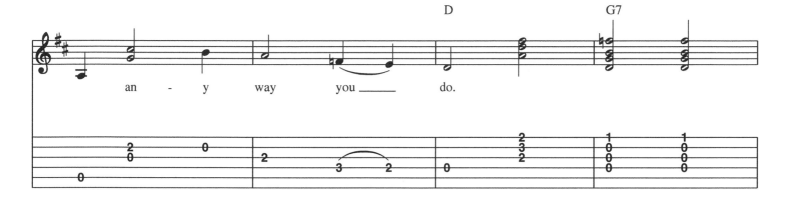

an - y way you _____ do.

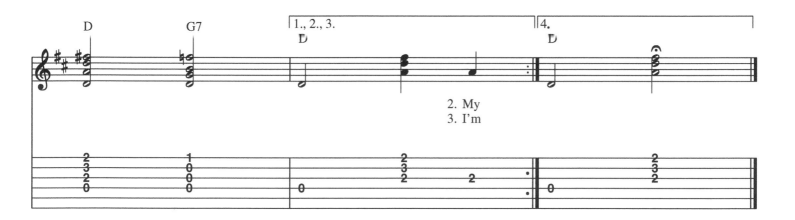

2. My
3. I'm

Additional Lyrics

3. I'm leavin' town now, baby,
   I'm leavin' town for sure.
   Then you won't be bothered with me
   hangin' round your door, but that's all (To Chorus)

4. I oughta mind my papa,
   Guess I'm not too smart.
   If I was I'd let you go
   Before you break my heart, but that's all (To Chorus)

Tutti Frutti

Words and Music by Little Richard Penniman and Dorothy La Bostrie

Verse

gal, ___ her name's Sue, she knows just what to do, ___ I got a

gal, ___ her name's Sue, ___ she knows just what to do. ___ I've

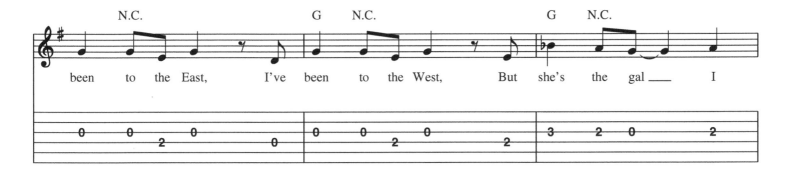

been to the East, I've been to the West, But she's the gal ___ I

love the best. __ Tut-ti gal for me. __ Tut-ti

lop, bop, boom!

Additional Lyrics

2. I got a gal, her name's Daisy,
She almost drives me crazy.
I got a gal, her name's Daisy,
She almost drives me crazy.
She's a real gone cookie, yes sir ree,
But pretty little Suzy's the gal for me.

What'd I Say

Words and Music by Ray Charles

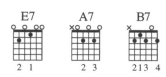

Strum Pattern: 2
Pick Pattern: 4

Intro

Bright Rock

Play 3 times

Verse

1. Hey, ma - ma, don't cha treat me ___ wrong. Come and love your dad - dy
2. – 5. *See additional lyrics*

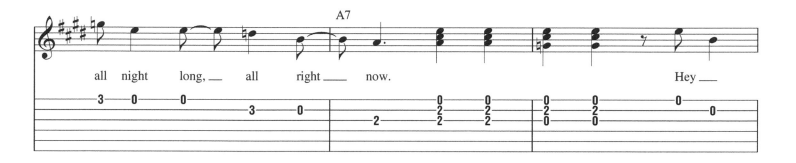

all night long, ___ all right ___ now. Hey ___

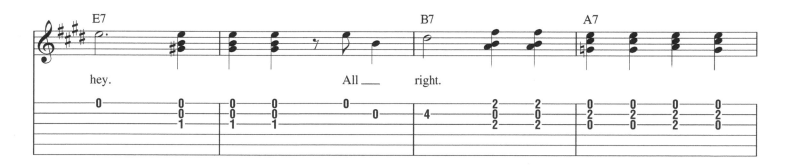

hey. All ___ right.

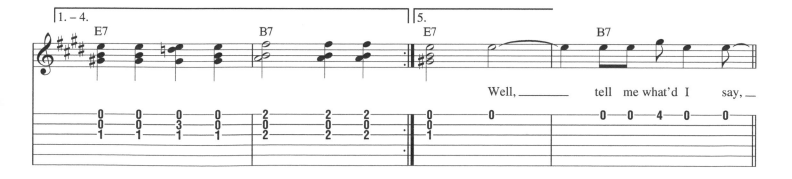

Well, ___ tell me what'd I say, ___

Outro

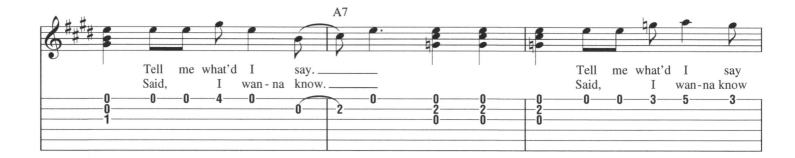

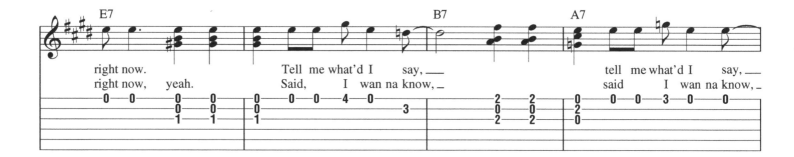

Additional Lyrics

2. See the girl with the diamond ring.
   She knows how to shake that thing.
   All right now. Hey, hey. Hey, hey.

3. Tell your mama, tell your pa.
   I'm gonna send you back to Arkansas.
   Oh yes, ma'm. You don't do right. Don't do right.

4. When you see me in misery,
   Come on, baby see about me now, yeah,
   Hey, hey. All right.

5. See the girl with the red dress on.
   She can do the birdland all night long.
   Oh yeah, yeah. What'd I say? All right.

Young Blood

Words and Music by Jerry Leiber, Mike Stoller and Doc Pomus

young blood _   I can't get you out of my mind. _____

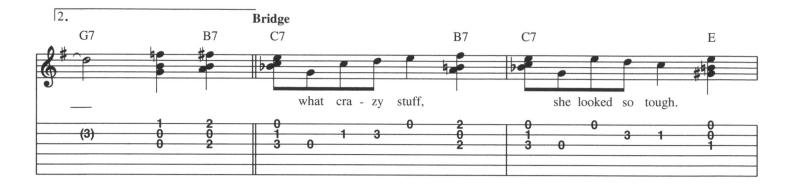

Bridge

_   what cra - zy stuff,   she looked so tough.

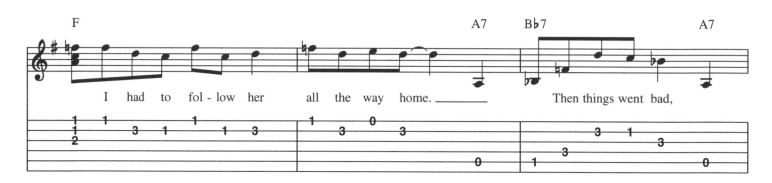

I had to fol - low her   all the way home. _____ Then things went bad,

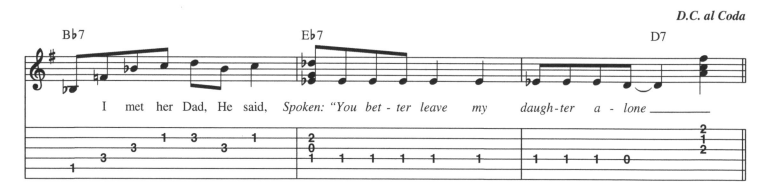

D.C. al Coda

I met her Dad, He said, *Spoken: "You bet - ter leave my daugh-ter a - lone* _____

✆ **Coda**

Outro-Chorus

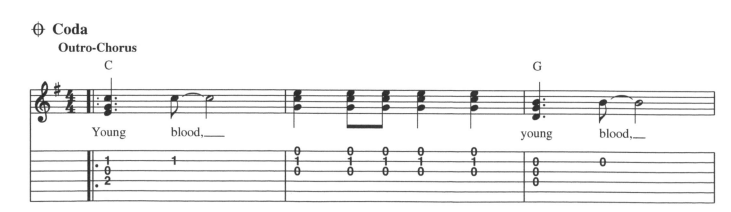

Young blood,___   young blood,___

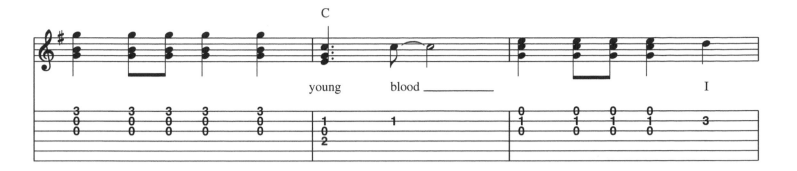

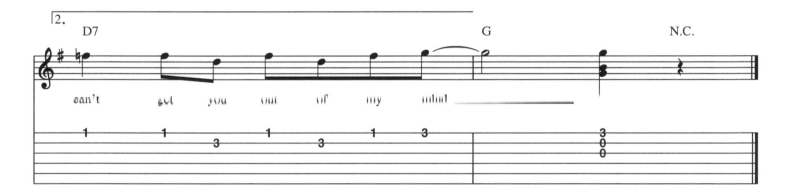

Additional Lyrics

2. I took one look and I was fractured.
   I tried to walk but I was lame.
   I tried to talk but I just stuttered,
   "What's your name, what's your name, what's your name, what's your name?"

3. I couldn't sleep a wink for trying.
   I saw the rising of the sun.
   And all night long my heart was crying,
   "You're the one, you're the one, you're the one, you're the one!"

Willie and the Hand Jive

Words and Music by Johnny Otis

A7   D7   E7

*Capo I

Strum Pattern: 6
Pick Pattern: 4

Intro
Moderately, in 2

Verse

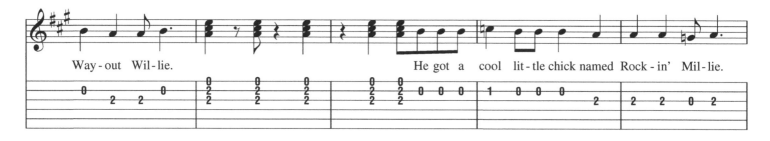

mf

1. I know a cat named
3. *See additional lyrics*

*Optional: To match recording, place capo at 1st fret.

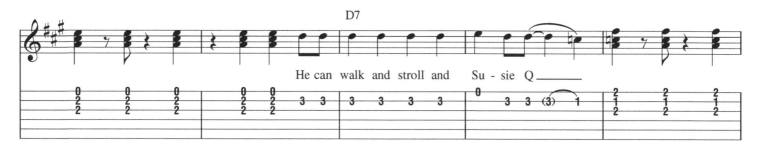

Way-out Wil-lie.   He got a   cool lit-tle chick named Rock-in' Mil-lie.

He can walk and stroll and   Su-sie Q _____

𝄋 Verse

and   do that cra-zy Hand _ Jive, too. _

2. Pa-pa told Wil-lie, "You'll
4., 5. *See additional lyrics*

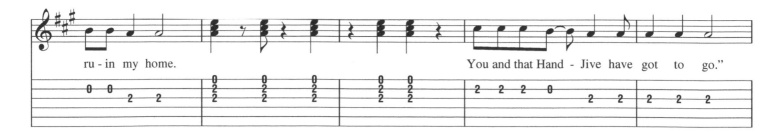

ru-in my home.   You and that Hand-Jive have got to   go."

Wil-lie said, "Pa - pa, don't put me down. ___

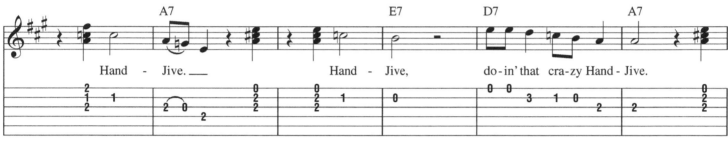

They're do-in' that Hand - Jive all o-ver town." ___ Hand - Jive,

Hand - Jive. ___ Hand - Jive, do-in' that cra-zy Hand - Jive.

To Coda ⊕

Guitar Solo

D.S. al Coda

⊕ **Coda**

Outro-Guitar Solo

Repeat and fade

Additional Lyrics

3. Mama, Mama, look at Uncle Joe.
   He's doin' the Hand-Jive with sister Flo.
   Grandma gave baby sister a dime.
   Said, "Do that Hand-Jive one more time."

4. Doctor and a lawyer and an Indian chief,
   Now they all dig that crazy beat.
   Way-Out Willie gave 'em all a treat
   When he did that Hand-Jive with his feet.

5. Now, Willie and Millie got married last fall.
   They had a little Willie Junior and that ain't all.
   Well, the baby got famous in his crib, you see,
   Doin' the Hand-Jive on TV.

This series features simplified arrangements with notes, tab, chord charts, and strum and pick patterns.

MIXED FOLIOS

00702287	Acoustic	$19.99
00702002	Acoustic Rock Hits for Easy Guitar	$15.99
00702166	All-Time Best Guitar Collection	$19.99
00702232	Best Acoustic Songs for Easy Guitar	$16.99
00119835	Best Children's Songs	$16.99
00703055	The Big Book of Nursery Rhymes & Children's Songs	$16.99
00698978	Big Christmas Collection	$19.99
00702394	Bluegrass Songs for Easy Guitar	$15.99
00289632	Bohemian Rhapsody	$19.99
00703387	Celtic Classics	$16.99
00224808	Chart Hits of 2016-2017	$14.99
00267383	Chart Hits of 2017-2018	$14.99
00334293	Chart Hits of 2019-2020	$16.99
00403479	Chart Hits of 2021-2022	$16.99
00702149	Children's Christian Songbook	$9.99
00702028	Christmas Classics	$8.99
00101779	Christmas Guitar	$14.99
00702141	Classic Rock	$8.95
00159642	Classical Melodies	$12.99
00253933	Disney/Pixar's Coco	$16.99
00702203	CMT's 100 Greatest Country Songs	$34.99
00702283	The Contemporary Christian Collection	$16.99

00196954	Contemporary Disney	$19.99
00702239	Country Classics for Easy Guitar	$24.99
00702257	Easy Acoustic Guitar Songs	$17.99
00702041	Favorite Hymns for Easy Guitar	$12.99
00222701	Folk Pop Songs	$17.99
00126894	Frozen	$14.99
00333922	Frozen 2	$14.99
00702286	Glee	$16.99
00702160	The Great American Country Songbook	$19.99
00702148	Great American Gospel for Guitar	$14.99
00702050	Great Classical Themes for Easy Guitar	$9.99
00275088	The Greatest Showman	$17.99
00148030	Halloween Guitar Songs	$14.99
00702273	Irish Songs	$14.99
00192503	Jazz Classics for Easy Guitar	$16.99
00702275	Jazz Favorites for Easy Guitar	$17.99
00702274	Jazz Standards for Easy Guitar	$19.99
00702162	Jumbo Easy Guitar Songbook	$24.99
00232285	La La Land	$16.99
00702258	Legends of Rock	$14.99
00702189	MTV's 100 Greatest Pop Songs	$34.99
00702272	1950s Rock	$16.99
00702271	1960s Rock	$16.99
00702270	1970s Rock	$24.99
00702269	1980s Rock	$16.99

00702268	1990s Rock	$24.99
00369043	Rock Songs for Kids	$14.99
00109725	Once	$14.99
00702187	Selections from O Brother Where Art Thou?	$19.99
00702178	100 Songs for Kids	$16.99
00702515	Pirates of the Caribbean	$17.99
00702125	Praise and Worship for Guitar	$14.99
00287930	Songs from *A Star Is Born, The Greatest Showman, La La Land*, and More Movie Musicals	$16.99
00702285	Southern Rock Hits	$12.99
00156420	Star Wars Music	$16.99
00121535	30 Easy Celtic Guitar Solos	$16.99
00244654	Top Hits of 2017	$14.99
00283786	Top Hits of 2018	$14.99
00302269	Top Hits of 2019	$14.99
00355779	Top Hits of 2020	$14.99
00374083	Top Hits of 2021	$16.99
00702294	Top Worship Hits	$17.99
00702255	VH1's 100 Greatest Hard Rock Songs	$34.99
00702175	VH1's 100 Greatest Songs of Rock and Roll	$34.99
00702253	Wicked	$12.99

ARTIST COLLECTIONS

00702267	AC/DC for Easy Guitar	$16.99
00156221	Adele – 25	$16.99
00396889	Adele – 30	$19.99
00702040	Best of the Allman Brothers	$16.99
00702865	J.S. Bach for Easy Guitar	$15.99
00702169	Best of The Beach Boys	$16.99
00702292	The Beatles — 1	$22.99
00125796	Best of Chuck Berry	$16.99
00702201	The Essential Black Sabbath	$15.99
00702250	blink-182 — Greatest Hits	$17.99
02501615	Zac Brown Band — The Foundation	$17.99
02501621	Zac Brown Band — You Get What You Give	$16.99
00702043	Best of Johnny Cash	$17.99
00702090	Eric Clapton's Best	$16.99
00702086	Eric Clapton — from the Album Unplugged	$17.99
00702202	The Essential Eric Clapton	$17.99
00702053	Best of Patsy Cline	$17.99
00222697	Very Best of Coldplay – 2nd Edition	$17.99
00702229	The Very Best of Creedence Clearwater Revival	$16.99
00702145	Best of Jim Croce	$16.99
00702278	Crosby, Stills & Nash	$12.99
14042809	Bob Dylan	$15.99
00702276	Fleetwood Mac — Easy Guitar Collection	$17.99
00139462	The Very Best of Grateful Dead	$16.99
00702136	Best of Merle Haggard	$16.99
00702227	Jimi Hendrix — Smash Hits	$19.99
00702288	Best of Hillsong United	$12.99
00702236	Best of Antonio Carlos Jobim	$15.99

00702245	Elton John — Greatest Hits 1970–2002	$19.99
00129855	Jack Johnson	$17.99
00702204	Robert Johnson	$16.99
00702234	Selections from Toby Keith — 35 Biggest Hits	$12.95
00702003	Kiss	$16.99
00702216	Lynyrd Skynyrd	$17.99
00702182	The Essential Bob Marley	$16.99
00146081	Maroon 5	$14.99
00121925	Bruno Mars – Unorthodox Jukebox	$12.99
00702248	Paul McCartney — All the Best	$14.99
00125484	The Best of MercyMe	$12.99
00702209	Steve Miller Band — Young Hearts (Greatest Hits)	$12.95
00124167	Jason Mraz	$15.99
00702096	Best of Nirvana	$16.99
00702211	The Offspring — Greatest Hits	$17.99
00138026	One Direction	$17.99
00702030	Best of Roy Orbison	$17.99
00702144	Best of Ozzy Osbourne	$14.99
00702279	Tom Petty	$17.99
00102911	Pink Floyd	$17.99
00702139	Elvis Country Favorites	$19.99
00702293	The Very Best of Prince	$19.99
00699415	Best of Queen for Guitar	$16.99
00109279	Best of R.E.M.	$14.99
00702208	Red Hot Chili Peppers — Greatest Hits	$17.99
00198960	The Rolling Stones	$17.99
00174793	The Very Best of Santana	$16.99
00702196	Best of Bob Seger	$16.99
00146046	Ed Sheeran	$17.99

00702252	Frank Sinatra — Nothing But the Best	$12.99
00702010	Best of Rod Stewart	$17.99
00702049	Best of George Strait	$17.99
00702259	Taylor Swift for Easy Guitar	$15.99
00359800	Taylor Swift – Easy Guitar Anthology	$24.99
00702260	Taylor Swift — Fearless	$14.99
00139727	Taylor Swift — 1989	$19.99
00115960	Taylor Swift — Red	$16.99
00253667	Taylor Swift — Reputation	$17.99
00702290	Taylor Swift — Speak Now	$16.99
00232849	Chris Tomlin Collection – 2nd Edition	$14.99
00702226	Chris Tomlin — See the Morning	$12.95
00148643	Train	$14.99
00702427	U2 — 18 Singles	$19.99
00702108	Best of Stevie Ray Vaughan	$17.99
00279005	The Who	$14.99
00702123	Best of Hank Williams	$15.99
00194548	Best of John Williams	$14.99
00702228	Neil Young — Greatest Hits	$17.99
00119133	Neil Young — Harvest	$14.99

Prices, contents and availability subject to change without notice.

Visit Hal Leonard online at **halleonard.com**